ILE

by Example

A Hands-on Guide
to the AS/400's
Integrated Language
Environment

MIKE CRAVITZ

 NEWS/400 Books™ is a division of
DUKE COMMUNICATIONS INTERNATIONAL

221 E. 29th Street • Loveland, CO 80538 USA
(800) 621-1544 • (970) 663-4700 • www.as400networkstore.com

Library of Congress Cataloging-in-Publication Data

Cravitz, Mike, 1946-
  ILE by example / by Mike Cravitz.
      p. cm.
Includes index.
  ISBN 1-58304-032-3
  1. IBM AS/400 (Computer)--Programming. 2. Programming languages
(Electronic computers) I. Title.
  QA76.8.I25919 C73 2000
  005.2'45--dc21

                                    00-009104

NEWS/400 Books™ is a division of
DUKE COMMUNICATIONS INTERNATIONAL
Loveland, Colorado USA

This book was printed and bound in Canada.

ISBN 1-58304-032-3

2002 2001 2000 WL 10 9 8 7 6 5 4 3 2 1

I dedicate this book to Philip and Becky.

I love you kids!

Well, you're not such kids anymore . . . .

Acknowledgments

I want to thank Richard Sweetman, Katie Tipton, Martha Nichols, Mike Friehauf, and Kathy Wong for their hard work in making this book possible. I want to extend a special thanks to Gary Guthrie for his thorough and thoroughly helpful comments regarding the manuscript. I want to thank Paul Conte, as well. Although Paul had nothing to do with this book, his mentoring approach to me at *NEWS/400* has helped me immensely in growing and learning. Finally, a special thanks to Tricia McConnell. Although she couldn't see this project to the end (through no fault of her own), she was very helpful in getting it started.

Table of Contents at a Glance

Table of Contents

Introduction

The learning process isn't always straightforward, and learning the AS/400's Integrated Language Environment (ILE) certainly was not a linear process for me. I recall the day back in 1994 when I first heard of ILE. I was doing some consulting work in Los Angeles, and an IBM representative arrived to help explain some of the new ILE concepts. He spent a solid hour answering questions, but it's not really possible to explain (or understand) in one hour the big picture of what's involved with ILE — much less the nuances of how to use it.

My understanding of ILE has progressed despite plenty of misconceptions and exaggerations I picked up along the way. Some of these mistakes resulted from my own incorrect thinking, and others I picked up by listening to other people who thought they understood how a particular aspect of ILE worked.

Although my understanding of ILE and its various advantages continues to grow, this book represents a culmination of this learning process. As you read, you'll find that I'm an opinionated cuss! However, I always try to support my opinion with facts. You may not always agree with my findings. I ask only that you consider my supporting material before arriving at your own opinions.

I want this book to present more than just theory, so I've included plenty of working examples to illustrate the book's concepts. The CD that accompanies this book contains all but the most trivial of the sample programs. Each source on the CD has explicit instructions regarding its use and any other sources that must be used in conjunction with it.

In Chapter 1, I address ILE program structure, which is quite different from the OPM program structure. In Chapter 2, I take up bind by copy. I not only explain this type of binding but also describe the (rare) situations in which this mechanism can be useful in your system design. Chapter 3 is devoted to ILE RPG subprocedures. Chapter 4 explains the very important and useful concept of a service program, including service program signatures. In Chapter 5, I demystify many aspects of activation groups and their use. A careful reading of this chapter will help you avoid common traps awaiting the typical ILE programmer. Chapter 6 helps you understand ILE exception handling and teaches you how to write your own ILE condition handler. Chapter 7 explains how you can use ILE cancel handlers to avoid various types of problems that can arise when your programs are canceled. Chapter 8 explains how to read and translate C prototypes into RPG prototypes so you can invoke C functions in an ILE RPG program.

Appendix A explains ILE optimization. Although the code in Appendices B and C isn't directly relevant to much of this book's content, it shows how you might use ILE RPG (and many of the techniques discussed in this book) to solve problems that you already face or will likely face in the future. Appendix D lists ILE-related AS/400 commands.

Note that I haven't included any information regarding the ILE debugger. Each of the ILE high-level languages has a unique set of issues with respect to the debugger. For this reason, IBM has included descriptions in each language's User's Guide about how to work with the debugger. These descriptions are quite well done. I urge you to read about the debugger in the User's Guides for whichever ILE languages you use.

Chapter 1

ILE Program Structure

One of the keys to the AS/400's survival has been the remarkable evolution of its *program models* — the set of interfaces and underlying processes that the machine interface (MI) and OS/400 provide to create and call programs and procedures. ILE is the latest program model to provide increased sophistication and flexibility to AS/400 programmers.

OPM, EPM, and ILE

When IBM introduced the AS/400 in 1988, it shipped the system with the Original Program Model (OPM), in which programs are always invoked dynamically. That is, when an OPM program invokes (usually via a Call statement) another program, the invoked program is located and loaded into memory at run time. Each program is a separate, independent object.

To facilitate the use of block-structured programming languages such as C and Pascal, IBM unofficially introduced the Extended Program Model (EPM) on the S/38 and made it official on the AS/400 with OS/400 V1R2. Several characteristics distinguish block-structured languages from traditional AS/400 languages such as RPG and Cobol, including

- the ability to define multiple blocks of code (sometimes referred to as *functions* or *procedures*) within a single source member with local variables (i.e., variables available only within the block) and the ability to receive parameters

- the ability to have local variables as well as variables that are available throughout a program or even across programs (i.e., flexible data scoping)

- multiple entry points within a single source member

IBM wanted to find a way to let traditional AS/400 languages such as RPG and Cobol also reap some of these benefits. But because IBM designed EPM as an extension to OPM, the EPM environment couldn't accomplish this task efficiently. So IBM developed an entirely separate model called the *Integrated Language Environment (ILE)* and introduced it in V2R3. Because ILE encompasses the functionality of EPM (and more) in a more efficient way, EPM is no longer considered a useful model for the AS/400.

Programs, Modules, and Procedures

One of the first things to learn about ILE is the composition of its program objects. Unlike the familiar OPM environment, in which a program is pretty much a single unit, ILE program objects are composed of *modules* written in any combination of participating languages — ILE RPG, ILE Cobol, ILE C, and ILE CL.

Figure 1.1 shows the relative complexity of an ILE program.

FIGURE 1.1

Anatomy of an ILE Program

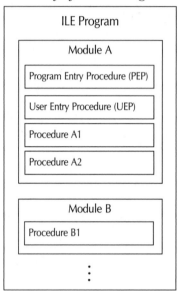

As you see, an ILE program consists of one or more modules; these modules, in turn, consist of *procedures*. The first module in an ILE program always consists of at least two procedures. One of them — the Program Entry Procedure (PEP) — is generated by the system and is always the first procedure to receive control in an ILE program. The first user-written procedure to receive control is called the User Entry Procedure (UEP). We'll see how the PEP and the UEP work in a moment.

Before V3R2 and V3R6, ILE RPG modules could contain only one user-written procedure. Now, however, we can create both a main procedure and subprocedures in an ILE RPG module.

To make these concepts a little more concrete, consider Figure 1.2. The figure shows two ILE RPG source members: Mod1 and Mod2. (Think of a module as an object that corresponds to a single compilable source member.) Mod1 calls the main procedure of module Mod2 using RPG's CallB (Call a Bound Procedure) opcode. To create a program from these two members, you must compile both source members into *Module objects using the CrtRpgMod (Create RPG Module) command. (CrtRpgMod is implemented as option 15 in Programming Development Manager, or PDM.) Then, you create an executable program using the CrtPgm (Create Program) command, specifying Module(Mod1 Mod2).

Note that the ILE RPG compiler (invoked via the CrtRpgMod command) doesn't produce a program object, as OPM compilers do. Instead, the ILE RPG compiler, as well as all other ILE compilers, produces modules — AS/400 objects of type *Module. A module is not executable. To create an executable object, you must combine one or more modules into an object of type *Pgm using the CrtPgm command.

FIGURE 1.2

Creating an ILE RPG Program Object

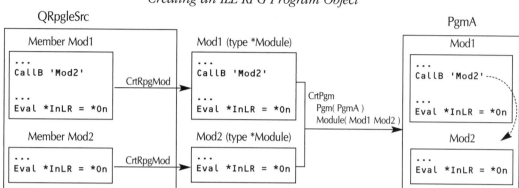

The CrtPgm command lets you specify the modules that make up an ILE program. One of CrtPgm's keywords, EntMod (Program Entry Procedure module), indicates which module is the first module to receive control when the program is invoked. By default, whichever module you specify first in the Module parameter is the entry point module. In Figure 1.2, Mod1 is the entry point module.

By the way, if your program contains only a single user-written module, you can use the CrtBndRpg (Create Bound RPG Program) command (option 14 in PDM) to perform module creation (CrtRpgMod) and program creation (CrtPgm) in a single step. The CrtBndRpg command automatically deletes the *Module object because in a single-module program, the module object isn't needed. These single-module programs are often referred to as *standalone* programs.

Upon execution of an ILE program, the first procedure to receive control is the PEP, as Figure 1.1 shows. The PEP doesn't correspond to any programming that the application programmer has coded; it's simply a system-generated procedure that receives control first. The PEP passes control to the UEP. In Figure 1.2, the UEP is the *main procedure* of Mod1. The main procedure is the initial part of an RPG module that we, the application developers, have written. Mod1 issues a CallB to Mod2. When you issue a CallB, control is transferred to the called procedure.

You might find it confusing that I refer to Mod2 here as "the called procedure" when, until now, I've called it a module. In reality, the CallB operation always invokes a procedure. Recall from our discussion of Figure 1.1 that modules consist of one or more procedures. Procedures are the potential entry points for a module. So we never actually invoke modules; we invoke procedures within modules. In the case of RPG, the name of the main procedure (or, more generically, the UEP) is always the same as the name of the module. So when Factor 2 of a CallB instruction is a module name, we are actually calling the main procedure.

Figures 1.3A and 1.3B show an actual working example that illustrates this point.

FIGURE 1.3A

Source for ILE RPG Module Mod1

```
D PrmInvoke        S               2
D   InvokeProc1    C                         'P1'
D   InvokeProc2    C                         'P2'
D   InvokeMod2     C                         'M2'

C       *Entry          Plist
C                       Parm                            PrmInvoke

C                       Select

C                       When      PrmInvoke = InvokeProc1
C                       CallB     'Proc1'

C                       When      PrmInvoke = InvokeProc2
C                       CallB     'Proc2'

C                       When      PrmInvoke = InvokeMod2
C                       CallB     'Mod2'

C                       EndSl

C                       Eval      *InLR = *On
```

FIGURE 1.3B

Source for ILE RPG Module Mod2

```
(A)  * Start of main procedure

D Proc1           PR
D Proc2           PR

D DummyFld        S               1

D Msg             C                         'You invoked the main procedure.'

C     Msg             Dsply                 DummyFld
C                     Eval      *InLR = *On

  * End of main procedure


(B)  * Start of Proc1
P Proc1           B                         Export
D Msg             C                         'You invoked Proc1'
C     Msg             Dsply                 DummyFld
P Proc1           E
  * End of Proc1


(C)  * Start of Proc2
P Proc2           B                         Export
D Msg             C                         'You invoked Proc2'
C     Msg             Dsply                 DummyFld
P Proc2           E
  * End of Proc2
```

Figure 1.3A shows the source for module Mod1, and Figure 1.3B shows the source for module Mod2. Let's assume we'll create from these two module objects a program object called PgmA. To do this, we take the steps shown in Figure 1.2. First, we use the CrtRpgMod command twice to create the module objects. Then, we use the CrtPgm command to bind the two modules together into a program object.

In the source for Mod2 in Figure 1.3B, the main procedure appears at **A**. In an ILE RPG program, the *main procedure* is the RPG code before the first subprocedure (if any). This module contains two subprocedures, Proc1 and Proc2, which appear at **B** and **C** (respectively) in the figure.

Tip

Unless you've been exposed to RPG subprocedures in the past, several elements in this source module are probably unfamiliar to you. Don't worry! You don't need to understand everything in the figure to grasp the points I'm making here.

In the main procedure at **A**, the first thing we see are some D-specs with a declaration type of PR. These are *prototype specifications.* I discuss prototypes in detail in Chapter 3; for now, you need to know only that these specifications are necessary whenever you have subprocedures defined in your module source. The only thing this main procedure does is use the RPG Dsply opcode to display a named constant called Msg. Msg is defined as 'You invoked the main procedure.' After the message is displayed, the main procedure terminates in the normal manner by setting on the LR indicator.

Subprocedure Proc1 at **B** is similar. It also displays a named constant called Msg. But in Proc1, Msg is defined as 'You invoked Proc1'. Similarly, subprocedure Proc2 displays the message 'You invoked Proc2'. So depending on which of these three procedures is invoked, the caller will see one of three appropriate messages displayed via the RPG Dsply opcode.

Now look at Mod1 in Figure 1.3A. This module contains only a main procedure that accepts a single two-character parameter. If you pass the value 'P1' or 'P2' for this parameter, Mod1 invokes procedure Proc1 or Proc2, respectively. If you pass 'M2', Mod1 invokes the main procedure. Recall that the name of the main procedure for an ILE RPG module is the same as the module name. Therefore, the name of the main procedure in module Mod2 is Mod2.

This example contains all the program elements we've discussed, including modules (Mod1 and Mod2) and procedures (Mod1, Mod2, Proc1, and Proc2). Module Mod1 has only a single user-written procedure that is the main procedure in the module. Mod2 has a main procedure and two other procedures: Proc1 and Proc2.

Note

With respect to RPG, the terms "procedure" and "subprocedure" refer to essentially the same thing. This text uses both terms.

ILE Programs and the Call Stack

Another important aspect of the ILE program structure relates to the call stack. In the OPM environment, a program occupies a single position on the call stack, but an ILE program doesn't occupy a position on the call stack per se. Instead, ILE procedures occupy positions on the call stack. Suppose I issue the following command on the AS/400 command line:

```
Call  PgmA Parm( P2 )
```

If we follow the program logic in Figures 1.3A and 1.3B, we see that the main procedure in Mod1 invokes Proc2 in Mod2. If we then freeze this execution at **C** in Mod2, the call stack would look something like Figure 1.4.

FIGURE **1.4**

The Call Stack While in Proc2 in PgmA

```
                          Display Call Stack
                                                  System:    S100B54R
    Job:   QPADEV0003    User:   MCRAVITZ    Number:   034509

    Thread:   0000020A

           Program
    Rqs    or
    Lvl    Procedure   Library    Statement         Instruction
           QCMD        QSYS                          0440
           QUICMENU    QSYS                          00C1
      1    QUIMNDRV    QSYS                          0502
      2    QUIMGFLW    QSYS                          04B5
      3    QUICMD      QSYS                          0411
           QUOCPP      QPDA                          063F
           QUOMAIN     QPDA                          00EA
      4    QUOCMD      QSYS                          01C2
         < P_PEP_MOD1  MCRAVITZ
           MOD1        MCRAVITZ   0000000035
           PROC2       MCRAVITZ   0000000043
```

The last three entries in the call stack in Figure 1.4 show the PEP for Mod1, the UEP for Mod1, and procedure Proc2. Let me reemphasize: these are all procedure entries on the call stack, not program entries. *In ILE, the executable entities in the call stack are always procedures.*

Figures 1.5A, 1.5B, and 1.5C show the displayable output that results from calling PgmA from an AS/400 command line and passing the allowable parameter values.

FIGURE 1.5A

Result of Call PgmA Parm('P1')

```
                        Display Program Messages
 DSPLY   You invoked Proc1


 Type reply, press Enter.
   Reply . . .   _____


 F3=Exit    F12=Cancel
```

FIGURE 1.5B

Result of Call PgmA Parm('P2')

```
                        Display Program Messages
 DSPLY   You invoked Proc2


 Type reply, press Enter.
   Reply . . .   _____


 F3=Exit    F12=Cancel
```

FIGURE 1.5C

Result of Call PgmA Parm('M2')

```
                        Display Program Messages
 DSPLY   You invoked the main procedure.


 Type reply, press Enter.
   Reply . . .   _____


 F3=Exit    F12=Cancel
```

Summary

ILE programs are built from separately compiled objects called *Module objects, which are composed of procedures. Every ILE program consists of (at least) a system-generated Program Entry Procedure (PEP) and a User Entry Procedure (UEP). In an ILE RPG program, the UEP is referred to as the *main procedure*. Other procedures in an ILE RPG module are called *subprocedures*.

Chapter 2

Bind by Copy

I explained in Chapter 1 that the output of an ILE compiler is not a program but a module. Each ILE compiler has a command for creating *standalone* programs — programs consisting of a single module. These are the CrtBnd*Xxx* commands, where *Xxx* stands for the particular language:

- CrtBndRpg (Create Bound RPG Program)
- CrtBndCbl (Create Bound Cobol Program)
- CrtBndCl (Create Bound CL Program)
- CrtBndC (Create Bound C Program)

You normally invoke these commands using option 14 in PDM.

If all your ILE programs are standalone, you can be lulled into thinking that compiling and binding are the same thing. However, the CrtBnd*Xxx* commands actually perform the work of two commands: Crt*Xxx*Mod (Create *Xxx* Module) and CrtPgm (Create Program). When you create standalone programs using CrtBnd*Xxx*, the *compiling* step (Crt*Xxx*Mod) creates a temporary module object that's deleted when the process is completed. Then, the *binding* step (CrtPgm) creates a program or service program from one or more modules. When more than one module is involved, the modules must be bound into a single executable object.

ILE permits two kinds of binding: bind by copy and bind by reference. You use bind by reference with service programs; this type of binding is the subject of Chapter 4. In this chapter, we're concerned with bind by copy. It's called *bind by copy* because the modules are actually copied wholesale into the program object.

Figure 2.1 (repeated from Chapter 1) shows the process of compiling and then binding two modules into an executable program. Notice that Mod1 and Mod2 are actually copied into the program object. That's why this process is called bind by *copy*. With this type of binding, Mod2 (and all its procedures) become part of the program object called PgmA in the figure. The ILE RPG CallB instruction invoking the main procedure in Mod2 will be considerably faster than a traditional dynamic call.

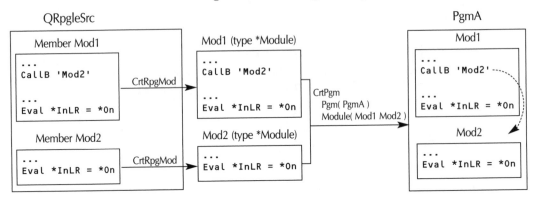

FIGURE 2.1
Creating an ILE RPG Program Object

Binding Directories

At first, managing ILE objects isn't a problem because they're few in number, but with time, the number of objects (and references to them with modular techniques) grows, and the task of identifying and managing the various pieces of your ILE applications can become an administrative burden.

IBM invented *binding directories* (AS/400 objects of type *BndDir) to help address the task of managing modules. A binding directory is simply a list of modules and service programs. One or more binding directories may be referenced in the CrtPgm command. Here's an example:

```
CrtPgm   Pgm( PgmX )
         Module( MainMod )
         BndDir( YourLib/ArBnd )
         ActGrp( *Caller )
```

When you reference a binding directory this way, the binder will examine the contents of the binding directory to resolve external references. For example, suppose module MainMod is an RPG module that contains the following instruction:

```
C                       CallB       'Mod1'
```

Because the CrtPgm command above doesn't specify which other modules to include, the binder will examine the binding directory (ArBnd in this example) to attempt to resolve this reference. So if you use a binding directory, you need to specify only the name of the main module in the Module parameter. The binder can find the rest of the modules in the binding directory.

You use the CrtBndDir (Create Binding Directory) command to create a binding directory. You might create your binding directory as follows:

```
CrtBndDir   YourLib/ArBnd
```

This command creates an empty binding directory. To add entries to a binding directory, you can use the AddBndDirE (Add Binding Directory Entry) command. But it's probably easier to use the WrkBndDirE (Work with Binding Directory Entries) command. So after creating binding directory ArBnd, you can work with binding directory entries by entering this command:

```
WrkBndDirE   BndDir( YourLib/ArBnd )
```

This command produces a screen like that shown in Figure 2.2A.

FIGURE 2.2A

Work with Binding Directory Entries Screen

```
                    Work with Binding Directory Entries

     Binding Directory:    ARBND          Library:    YOURLIB

     Type options, press Enter.
       1=Add    4=Remove

                                                --------Creation---------
     Opt      Object        Type          Library      Date         Time
      _      _____     _____      _____

       (No binding directory entries for this binding directory.)




                                                                    Bottom
     Parameters or command
     ===> _____
     F3=Exit    F4=Prompt    F9=Retrieve    F5=Refresh    F12=Cancel    F17=Top
     F18=Bottom
```

As the screen shows, you can use option 1 to add a binding directory entry and option 4 to remove one. Figure 2.2B shows how you must fill in this screen to add a module called Mod1 to the ArBnd binding directory, and Figure 2.2C shows the screen after you've added Mod1.

FIGURE 2.2B
Adding a New Entry to the Binding Directory

```
                    Work with Binding Directory Entries

   Binding Directory:    ARBND          Library:    YOURLIB

   Type options, press Enter.
     1=Add    4=Remove

                                              --------Creation---------
   Opt     Object        Type      Library    Date          Time
    1      Mod1_____    *Module   _____
      (No binding directory entries for this binding directory.)




                                                                Bottom
   Parameters or command
   ===> _____
   F3=Exit    F4=Prompt    F9=Retrieve    F5=Refresh    F12=Cancel    F17=Top
   F18=Bottom
```

FIGURE 2.2C
Binding Directory After Adding a Module

```
                    Work with Binding Directory Entries

   Binding Directory:    ARBND          Library:    YOURLIB

   Type options, press Enter.
     1=Add    4=Remove

                                              --------Creation---------
   Opt     Object        Type      Library    Date          Time
    _      _____
    _      MOD1          *MODULE   *LIBL      04/14/00      13:20:20




                                                                Bottom
   Parameters or command
   ===> _____
   F3=Exit    F4=Prompt    F9=Retrieve    F5=Refresh    F12=Cancel    F17=Top
   F18=Bottom
```

Notice that the Type field is specified as *Module. There are two object types you can put into a binding directory: *Module (module) and *SrvPgm (service program).

When you reference a binding directory in the CrtPgm command, the binder will pick up only the modules and service programs it needs to resolve the various references in the program. In our example, if the only unresolved reference in MainMod is the bound call to procedure Mod1 (which is the main procedure in module Mod1), the binder will pick up only 'Mod1' from the binding directory. In other words, even if the binding directory has thousands of entries in it, the binder will use only the entries it needs. This means you can include several module and service program names in the binding directory. One effective strategy is to create a binding directory that includes the names of all the modules and service programs in an entire application, such as order entry or accounts payable. This simplifies the management of modules when using bind by copy.

So how can we keep track of the names of the main modules? One possibility is to give your main modules the same name as, or a name easily derived from, the program name. This approach requires you to keep track of only your program names for the purpose of binding. Whatever approach you choose, you can see why binding directories can be helpful when using bind by copy — and they're just as useful for keeping track of service programs.

Factors to Consider When Using Bind by Copy

Should you always decompose your application into small, manageable modules and use bind by copy? Not necessarily! Certainly, it's usually a good idea to decompose an application into small, well-defined "chunks" of code. But should these chunks necessarily be ILE objects? Let's consider some of the problems associated with using bind by copy.

Suppose I need to make a small change to a module called Sub1, which is bound by copy into 500 programs. This means I must recompile Sub1 and then rebind it to 500 programs. And that's not the only problem; there are performance implications as well. Imagine that during an average peak hour (perhaps 2:00 p.m. to 3:00 p.m.), an average of 30 of these 500 programs are in concurrent use. Because Sub1 is bound by copy into these programs, there are potentially 30 copies of Sub1 consuming memory resources during an average peak hour. In summary, indiscriminate use of bind by copy can lead to these problems:

- the need to rebind when a change is made and, therefore, …
- the need to use a good impact analysis and/or change management tool to determine which programs use the recompiled module
- the need to allocate the time and other resources necessary to rebind the affected programs
- inefficient memory utilization

Don't get me wrong; I'm not suggesting that you shouldn't own and use a good impact analysis or change management tool. However, in this case, there are two good alternatives to bind by copy: bind by reference with service programs and dynamic call.

If you have a module that's needed by multiple programs, it's usually best to include that module in a service program. I discuss service programs in detail in Chapter 4. But, returning to our hypothetical Sub1 module, suppose that only a single program needs Sub1. In this case, it makes no sense to place Sub1 in a service program, and none of the bind-by-copy problems that I cited apply — so I should use bind by copy, right? Not necessarily. There's a third option: good old-fashioned dynamic bind. In other words, I can compile Sub1 as a standalone program and simply call it the way I always did in OPM. Dynamic call is far slower than a static call, but this isn't always an important consideration. And despite being slower, dynamic call has certain advantages. For example, it leaves you fewer objects to manage than bind by copy does.

The primary advantage with bind by copy is a faster call. So let's analyze how much faster the call is. Figures 2.3A, 2.3B, and 2.3C show the source for a program called Pgm02 that analyzes the difference between using dynamic call and static call where the static call uses bind by copy.

Figure 2.3A
ILE RPG Module SrcA

```
********************************************************************
*
* Module Name: SrcA
*
* This module compares static and dynamic call. It accepts
* a parameter that tells it how many calls to make. It
* calls and times (to the nearest second) that many static
* calls to SrcB as well as SrcC. It then displays information
* about the difference between the two techniques.
*
* Compile this and SrcB with PDM option 15. Compile SrcC with
* PDM option 14. Issue the following command...
*
* CrtPgm  Pgm( Pgm02 ) Module( SrcA SrcB ) ActGrp( *Caller )
*
* To run a test, call this program from the command, line passing
* a single numeric parameter. For example, to run a test
* with 500,000 calls, invoke this program from the command
* line as follows:
*
*   Call  Pgm02 500000
*
********************************************************************


 * Prototypes
D CurrCpuMsecs    PR            10I 0
D   DummyPrm                     1     Options( *Omit )

 * Data used in program
D NumCalls        S             11P 0
D StatElpTime     S             10I 0
D DynElpTime      S             10I 0
D DynStrCpuTime   S             10I 0
D DynEndCpuTime   S             10I 0
D StatStrCpuTime  S             10I 0
D StatEndCpuTime  S             10I 0
```

continued

FIGURE 2.3A *CONTINUED*

```
D OneMinuteDiff    S              9P 0
D Dummy            S              1
D AbsoluteDiff     S              8F
D DiffPerCall      S              8F
D DpcPacked        S              11P10
D Msg              S              51

 * Parameter definition
D PrmNumCalls      S              15P 5

C     *Entry       Plist
C                  Parm                        PrmNumCalls

 * Convert the 15,5 parameter to an 11,0 field
C                  Eval      NumCalls = PrmNumCalls

 * Time static calls
C                  Eval      StatStrCpuTime = CurrCpuMsecs( *Omit )
C                  Do        NumCalls
C                  CallB     'SrcB'
C                  EndDo
C                  Eval      StatEndCpuTime = CurrCpuMsecs( *Omit )
C                  Eval (H)  StatElpTime =   ( StatEndCpuTime
C                                          -   StatStrCpuTime )
C                                          / 1000

 * Time dynamic calls
C                  Eval      DynStrCpuTime = CurrCpuMsecs( *Omit )
C                  Do        NumCalls
C                  Call      'SrcC'
C                  EndDo
C                  Eval      DynEndCpuTime = CurrCpuMsecs( *Omit )
C                  Eval (H)  DynElpTime =    ( DynEndCpuTime
C                                          -   DynStrCpuTime )
C                                          / 1000

 * Subtract these two elapsed times to get the absolute difference
C                  Eval      AbsoluteDiff = DynElpTime - StatElpTime

 * Divide by the number of calls to get the difference per call
C                  Eval      DiffPerCall = AbsoluteDiff / NumCalls

 * Divide 60 by above result to get number of seconds to make
 * one minute difference
C                  Eval (H)  OneMinuteDiff = 60 / DiffPerCall

 * Report results
C                  Eval      Msg =
C                              %Trim( %EditC( NumCalls: 'J' ) )
C                            + ' dynamic calls took '
C                            + %Trim( %EditC( DynElpTime: 'J' ) )
C                            + ' seconds.'
C     Msg          Dsply
C                  Eval      Msg =
C                              %Trim( %EditC( NumCalls: 'J' ) )
```

continued

FIGURE 2.3A *CONTINUED*

```
C                                + ' static calls took '
C                                + %Trim( %EditC( StatElpTime: 'J' ) )
C                                + ' seconds.'
C        Msg           Dsply

C                      Eval      DpcPacked = DiffPerCall
C                      Eval      Msg =
C                                  'Difference in seconds per call = '
C                                + %Trim( %EditC( DpcPacked: 'J'    ) )
C                                + '.'
C        Msg           Dsply

C                      Eval      Msg =
C                                  %Trim( %EditC( OneMinuteDiff: 'J' ) )
C                                + ' calls req''d to make '
C                                + '1 minute''s difference.'
C        Msg           Dsply                    Dummy

C                      Eval      *InLR = *On
 * = * = * = * = * = * = * = * = * = * = * = * = * = * = * = * =
 * CurrCpuMsecs - Returns the CPU utilization of this job in
 *               milliseconds
P CurrCpuMsecs    B

D CurrCpuMsecs    PI              10I 0
D  DummyPrm                        1    Options( *Omit )

 * Local variables
D GetJobInf       PR                      ExtPgm( 'QUSRJOBI' )
D  GjiOutputInf                  100
D  GjiLenOf...
D   OutputInf                     10I 0 Const
D  GjiFmtName                      8    Const
D  GjiQlJobName                   26    Const
D  GjiIntJobId                    16    Const

D JobInf          DS
D  JiBytesRetd                    10I 0
D  JiBytesAvl                     10I 0
D  JiCpuMsecs              97    100B 0

 * Initialize the bytes available field in the JobInf data structure
C                      Eval      JiBytesAvl = %Size( JobInf )

 * Invoke the QUSRJOBI API to retrieve the current CPU
 * utilization in milliseconds
C                      CallP     GetJobInf( JobInf:
C                                           %Size( JobInf ):
C                                           'JOBI0150':
C                                           '*':
C                                           *Blank )

C                      Return    JiCpuMsecs

P CurrCpuMsecs    E
```

FIGURE 2.3B
ILE RPG Module SrcB

```
********************************************************************
*
* Module Name: SrcB
*
* Used in generating Pgm02.
*
* Compile this and SrcA with PDM option 15. Compile SrcC with
* PDM option 14. Issue the following command...
*
* CrtPgm  Pgm( Pgm02 ) Module( SrcA SrcB ) ActGrp( *Caller )
*
* To run a test, call Pgm02 from the command line, passing
* a single numeric parameter. For example, to run a test
* with 500,000 calls, invoke this program from the command
* line as follows:
*
*   Call  Pgm02 500000
*
********************************************************************
C                   Return
```

FIGURE 2.3C
ILE RPG Module SrcC

```
********************************************************************
*
* Module Name: SrcC
*
* Used in generating Pgm02.
*
* Compile SrcA and SrcB with PDM option 15. Compile SrcC with
* PDM option 14. Issue the following command...
*
* CrtPgm  Pgm( Pgm02 ) Module( SrcA SrcB ) ActGrp( *Caller )
*
* To run a test, call Pgm02 from the command line, passing
* a single numeric parameter. For example, to run a test
* with 500,000 calls, invoke this program from the command
* line as follows:
*
*   Call  Pgm02 500000
*
********************************************************************
C                   Return
```

I ran this program on my RISC AS/400 running OS/400 V4R3. The machine is pretty much a bottom-of-the-line P150 with 64 MB of main memory and 4 GB of disk.

Pgm02 accepts a single numeric parameter that specifies the number of calls to test. In my case, I used 500,000 calls. Pgm02 performs that many dynamic calls and an equal number of static calls. The procedures called are basically do-nothing procedures — an

RPG Return instruction. It's not necessary to time procedures that perform significant work because we're studying only the speed of the call. Pgm02 times both sets of calls and then displays the following information:

- the total amount of time in CPU seconds to make that many dynamic calls
- the total amount of time in CPU seconds to make that many static calls
- the difference between these two techniques per call (in fractions of a second)
- the number of calls required to produce one minute of difference between the static and dynamic calls

(Note that Pgm02 uses CPU utilization, rather than elapsed wall-clock time, to do its timing; this means you can obtain valid results even if you're running on a busy system.)

To invoke Pgm02, I issued the following command from the AS/400 command line:

```
Call  Pgm02 500000
```

Figure 2.4 shows the output I received from this program.

FIGURE 2.4
Output Received from Program Pgm02

```
                    Display Program Messages

  DSPLY   500,000 dynamic calls took 105 seconds.
  DSPLY   500,000 static calls took 6 seconds.
  DSPLY   Difference in seconds per call = .0001979999.
  DSPLY   303,030 calls req'd to make 1 minute's difference.







  Type reply, press Enter.
    Reply . . .
    _____
    _____

  F3=Exit    F12=Cancel
```

The figure shows that 500,000 dynamic calls required 105 CPU seconds. The same number of static calls required only 6 seconds. If you end your analysis here, you might believe that static call is so much faster that you should never use dynamic call. But the third and fourth lines of output from this program give us a deeper, more meaningful analysis.

The third line tells us that the difference per call between using dynamic and static is approximately 0.0002 seconds or 2/10,000 seconds. This fact helps us analyze whether it's important to use bind by copy rather than dynamic bind in an interactive application. A typical function in an interactive application isn't called very many times — perhaps a maximum of 50 times. (In fact, if you need to make more than 50 calls to a particular program or module in an interactive application, you should probably consider running the function in batch.) So, assuming you're making 50 calls, the difference between dynamic call and static call would be 50 calls times 0.0002 seconds per call or 0.01 seconds. The interactive user probably won't perceive this difference. What's more, this analysis applies to my slower machine. On a larger machine than mine, these numbers will shrink accordingly.

Because bind by copy introduces additional management headaches, and because the amount of time it saves in most cases is insignificant, I don't recommend its use for interactive applications. So, let's turn our attention to batch applications.

The fourth line of output in Figure 2.4 can help us to analyze the batch situation. It says you must make approximately 300,000 calls to realize a one-minute time difference between dynamic call and static call. Stated another way, your batch job should take about one minute longer if you make 300,000 dynamic calls rather than static calls. Remember: this 300,000 number goes up in most cases if you're using a faster processor than mine. Also, I ran my test on a machine with one user job. If you have other activity, your results will vary from mine. Nevertheless, it's a fairly good guideline to expect that a standalone batch job that makes 300,000 calls on my machine will take about one CPU minute longer if those calls are dynamic than if they're static. After you run Pgm02 on your system, you must decide based on expected number of calls and your batch window whether this performance difference is significant to you. In most (but not all) cases, I believe using bind by copy in a batch system is also unnecessary.

Summary

Bind by copy is so named because the system literally copies the *Module objects into the program object. The process requires you to first compile your source into *Module objects and then "knit" these objects together using the CrtPgm command. Binding directories can help you manage modules when using bind by copy.

Using bind by copy results in a fast call, but the performance gain is seldom significant enough to warrant its use. If procedures in a module are invoked from multiple programs, that module is a good candidate for incorporation into a service program (bind by reference) instead of bind by copy. If a module is invoked from a single program, it's usually better to create a standalone program and invoke the module dynamically. One exception to this rule is a batch application in which the module is being called a sufficient number of times to cause a performance problem with respect to your installation's batch windows. I outline another exception to the no-bind-by-copy rule in Chapter 3 on RPG subprocedures. However, as you'll see, this exception is rare. For the most part, I believe the best course is to avoid bind by copy.

Chapter 3

ILE RPG Subprocedures

Let's begin this discussion of RPG subprocedures with some observations about RPG subroutines. First of all, RPG subroutines have two basic uses: decomposition and service.

Most programs have enough inherent complexity that it behooves us to split the work of a program into smaller, more manageable chunks, which RPG programmers have traditionally implemented as subroutines. These subroutines are invoked from a single location (via the ExSr, or Execute Subroutine, operation) within the source. I call this type of subroutine a *decomposition* of the program because it is used to decompose a complex problem into smaller problems.

A *service* subroutine performs some sort of general service — such as an interest calculation — on behalf of the rest of a program. A service subroutine is potentially invoked from multiple locations within a program.

I distinguish these two uses for a subroutine because I want to point out that service subroutines (and not decomposition subroutines) make the best candidates for RPG subprocedures. In the discussion that follows, I use the term "RPG subroutine" to refer to RPG service subroutines.

Illustrating Subprocedures with the Personal Planning Application

RPG subprocedures offer several advantages over RPG subroutines. To illustrate some of these advantages, I'll walk you through a small personal planner program that first uses a subroutine to perform an interest calculation and then uses an RPG subprocedure to perform the same task. Figures 3.1A and 3.1B show the workings of the personal planner program.

As you can see, this program calculates monthly payments for an auto loan and a mortgage. For the purposes of this illustration, I've assumed both loans are calculated the same way, using standard formulas for computing an even monthly payment on a declining balance.[1]

---

1   Here is the mathematical formula I used to calculate the monthly payments:

$$M = (P * I) / (1 - (1 + I) ** -N)$$

where M = the calculated monthly payment; P = the loan principal; I = the monthly interest rate (yearly interest rate divided by 12 — for example, if I = 0.0075, the monthly interest rate is 0.75 percent and the yearly interest rate is 9 percent); and N = the number of equal monthly payments.

FIGURE 3.1A

Interest Calculator Before User Input

```
 6/02/00                    Personal Planner                  MCRAVITZ
 05:46:04                                                      S100B54R

 For Your Auto Loan...

   Amount Financed:                        .00
   Yearly Interest:                        .00     (e.g., 7.5 = 7.5 percent)
   Number of Equal
   Monthly Payments:               0

      Auto Loan Monthly Payment----------------      .00


 For Your Mortgage Loan...

   Amount Financed:                        .00
   Yearly Interest:                        .00     (e.g., 7.5 = 7.5 percent)
   Number of Equal
   Monthly Payments:               0

      Mortgage Monthly Payment----------------      .00

      F3=Exit
```

FIGURE 3.1B

Interest Calculator Showing User Input

```
 6/02/00                    Personal Planner                  MCRAVITZ
 05:46:04                                                      S100B54R

 For Your Auto Loan...

   Amount Financed:                  18,370.00
   Yearly Interest:                       7.25    (e.g., 7.5 = 7.5 percent)
   Number of Equal
   Monthly Payments:              36

      Auto Loan Monthly Payment----------------      569.31


 For Your Mortgage Loan...

   Amount Financed:                 150,000.00
   Yearly Interest:                       7.00    (e.g., 7.5 = 7.5 percent)
   Number of Equal
   Monthly Payments:             360

      Mortgage Monthly Payment----------------      997.95

      F3=Exit
```

Now let's examine Figures 3.2A and 3.2B, which show the DDS for the display file IntD and the ILE RPG interest-calculating program IntSub, respectively.

FIGURE 3.2A
Display File IntD

```
A                                    DSPSIZ(24 80 *DS3)
A           R R01
A                                    CA03(03)
A                               1  3DATE
A                                    EDTCDE(Y)
A                                    COLOR(WHT)
A                               1 69USER
A                                    COLOR(WHT)
A                               2  3TIME
A                                    COLOR(WHT)
A                               2 69SYSNAME
A                                    COLOR(WHT)
A                               1 33'Personal Planner'
A                                    COLOR(WHT)
A                               4  2'For Your Auto Loan...'
A                               6  4'Amount Financed:'
A           AUPRNCPL   11Y 2B   6 31EDTCDE(J)
A                                    COMP(GE 0.00)
A                               7  4'Yearly Interest:'
A           AUYRINT     5Y 2B   7 39EDTCDE(J)
A                                    COMP(GE 0.00)
A                               7 50'(e.g., 7.5 = 7.5 percent)'
A                               8  4'Number of Equal'
A                               9  4'Monthly Payments:'
A           AUNOPMTS    3Y 0B   9 39EDTCDE(J)
A                                    COMP(GE 0)
A                              11  6'Auto Loan Monthly Payment----------
A                                    -------'
A           AUPMT      11Y 20  11 48EDTCDE(J)
A                              15  2'For Your Mortgage Loan...'
A                              17  4'Amount Financed:'
A           MOPRNCPL   11Y 2B  17 31EDTCDE(J)
A                                    COMP(GE 0.00)
A                              18  4'Yearly Interest:'
A           MOYRINT     5Y 2B  18 39EDTCDE(J)
A                                    COMP(GE 0.00)
A                              18 50'(e.g., 7.5 = 7.5 percent)'
A                              19  4'Number of Equal'
A                              20  4'Monthly Payments:'
A           MONOPMTS    3Y 0B  20 39EDTCDE(J)
A                                    COMP(GE 0)
A                              22  6'Mortgage Monthly Payment----------
A                                    -------'
A           MOPMT      11Y 20  22 48EDTCDE(J)
A                              24  6'F3=Exit'
A                                    COLOR(BLU)
```

FIGURE 3.2B
ILE RPG Program IntSub

```
FIntD       CF   E               WorkStn

     * Program variables
(A)  D SuPrncpl        S                    Like( AuPrncpl )
     D SuYrInt         S                    Like( AuYrInt  )
     D SuNoPmts        S                    Like( AuNoPmts )
     D SuPmt           S                    Like( AuPmt    )

(B)  D SuMnthlyInt     S              8F

     * Loop until user presses the F3 key
     C                 DoU      *IN03 = *On

     C                 ExFmt    R01

     C                 If       *IN03 = *On
     C                 Leave
     C                 EndIf

     C                 If          AuPrncpl > *Zero
     C                 And AuYrInt   > *Zero
     C                 And AuNoPmts > *Zero

(C)  C                 Z-Add    AuPrncpl        SuPrncpl
     C                 Z-Add    AuYrInt         SuYrInt
     C                 Z-Add    AuNoPmts        SuNoPmts
     C                 ExSr     CalcMnthlyPmt
     C                 Z-Add    SuPmt           AuPmt

     C                 Else
     C                 Z-Add    *Zero           AuPmt

     C                 EndIf

     C                 If          MoPrncpl > *Zero
     C                 And MoYrInt   > *Zero
     C                 And MoNoPmts > *Zero

(D)  C                 Z-Add    MoPrncpl        SuPrncpl
     C                 Z-Add    MoYrInt         SuYrInt
     C                 Z-Add    MoNoPmts        SuNoPmts
     C                 ExSr     CalcMnthlyPmt
     C                 Z-Add    SuPmt           MoPmt

     C                 Else
     C                 Z-Add    *Zero           MoPmt

     C                 EndIf

     C                 EndDo

     C                 Eval     *INLR = *On
```

continued

FIGURE 3.2B CONTINUED

```
* = * = * = * = * = * = * = * = * = * = * = * = * = * = * = * =        (E)
* CalcMnthlyPmt subroutine - Calculate a monthly payment given
*                            principal, interest, and number of
*                            equal monthly payments
C     CalcMnthlyPmt BegSr

* Calculate the fractional value for monthly interest
* = to the yearly interest percent divided by 1200 (1200 = 12 months
* times 100 percent)
C                   Eval        SuMnthlyInt = SuYrInt / 1200

* Use the formula m = (pi/(1 - (1 + i)**-n) to compute the
* monthly interest. Note this computes an equal monthly
* payment for an interest amount applied to a declining
* balance.

C                   Eval (H)  SuPmt =    (    SuPrncpl * SuMnthlyInt )
C                             / (   1
C                                 - ( 1 + SuMnthlyInt ) ** -SuNoPmts )

C                   EndSr
```

Subroutine CalcMnthlyPmt at **E** in Figure 3.2B performs the standard calculation. This subroutine is invoked from two places (**C** and **D**) and has both input parameters and output parameters. Because RPG has no support for parameters in its subroutines, I had to designate ordinary fields to act as simulated parameters for subroutine CalcMnthlyPmt. These fields are defined at **A**. Subroutine CalcMnthlyPmt takes three simulated input parameters (SuPrncpl, SuYrInt, and SuNoPmts) and produces a monthly payment in its simulated output parameter (SuPmt). Note: At **C** and **D,** I use three Z-Add instructions to set the simulated input parameters before the ExSr operation, and I use another Z-Add after the ExSr to send the calculated monthly payment to its correct destination.

Also, the field SuMnthlyInt defined at **B** is actually intended to be used solely by the CalcMnthlyPmt subroutine. But because RPG data is global, nothing prevents a future maintenance programmer from using this variable somewhere else in the program, thus violating the original programmer's intent of defining a variable that's supposed to be local to this subroutine.

There's a third problem associated with RPG subroutines that this example doesn't illustrate. Because a subroutine's name must fit within Factor 2 of an ExSr statement, the name is limited to 14 characters. Sometimes, 14 characters isn't enough to properly name a subroutine. For example, assume I have two subroutines; one calculates vacation time for hourly employees, and the other calculates vacation time for salaried employees. To distinguish these two subroutines from each other, I'd like to name them as follows:

CalcSalEmpVac
CalcHourlyEmpVac

Although the first name is okay, the second exceeds the 14-character limit. I could abbreviate the word "Hourly" to something like "Hrly," but that wouldn't be as readable. Moreover, it's always preferable to have a standard set of abbreviations that your shop adheres to consistently. If I must limit name sizes, I can't really adhere to a set of standard abbreviation names because I can't always fit them inside the full name.

Let's summarize the problems presented by RPG subroutines.

- They don't have real parameters, so we must simulate parameters by using suitable assignment operations (such as Move, MoveL, Z-Add, and Eval) before and after invoking the subroutine.
- There's no way to limit to a particular subroutine the use of variables that are intended to be used only by that subroutine (i.e., there's no local variable support).
- Names are limited to 14 characters.

RPG subprocedures address all three of these issues (and others).

Figure 3.3 shows the source for RPG program IntProc, which uses subprocedures to perform exactly the same function as program IntSub in Figure 3.2B.

There are some things to watch out for when coding subprocedures. First, notice that the F-spec for display file IntD appears in the main procedure (just before **A**). F-specs can be coded only in the main procedure, and file fields are always globally available throughout the module. Also, you can't escape into the RPG cycle from a subprocedure. You can turn on the LR indicator in a subprocedure, but doing so will have no effect because when the subprocedure ends, you return to the invoking procedure rather than to the RPG cycle.

FIGURE 3.3
ILE RPG Program IntProc

```
FIntD       CF    E             WorkStn
```

(A)
```
  * Prototype
D MnthlyPmt      PR                     Like( AuPmt )
D  MiPrncpl                             Like( AuPrncpl )
D  MiYrInt                              Like( AuYrInt   )
D  MiNoPmts                             Like( AuNoPmts )
  * Loop until user presses the F3 key
C                     DoU       *IN03 = *On

C                     ExFmt     R01

C                     If        *IN03 = *On
C                     Leave
C                     EndIf

C                     If              AuPrncpl > *Zero
C                               And AuYrInt   > *Zero
C                               And AuNoPmts > *Zero
```

continued

FIGURE 3.3 *CONTINUED*

```
C                    Eval      AuPmt = MnthlyPmt( AuPrncpl:          (B)
C                                                AuYrInt:
C                                                AuNoPmts )

C                    Else
C                    Z-Add     *Zero           AuPmt

C                    EndIf

C                    If              MoPrncpl > *Zero
C                              And MoYrInt   > *Zero
C                              And MoNoPmts > *Zero

C                    Eval      MoPmt = MnthlyPmt( MoPrncpl:          (C)
C                                                MoYrInt:
C                                                MoNoPmts )

C                    Else
C                    Z-Add     *Zero           MoPmt

C                    EndIf

C                    EndDo

C                    Eval      *INLR = *On

 * = * = * = * = * = * = * = * = * = * = * = * = * = * = * = * =
 * MnthlyPmt procedure   - Calculate a monthly payment given
 *                         principal, interest, and number of
 *                         equal monthly payments
P MnthlyPmt        B                                                (D)

D MnthlyPmt        PI                  Like( AuPmt )                (E)
D  MiPrncpl                            Like( AuPrncpl )
D  MiYrInt                             Like( AuYrInt  )
D  MiNoPmts                            Like( AuNoPmts )

 * Local variables
D MiMnthlyInt      S               8F
 * Calculate the fractional value for monthly interest
 * = to the yearly interest percent divided by 1200 (1200 = 12 months
 * times 100 percent)
C                    Eval      MiMnthlyInt = MiYrInt / 1200

 * Use the formula m = (pi/(1 - (1 + i)**-n) to compute the
 * monthly interest. Note this computes an equal monthly
 * payment for an interest amount applied to a declining
 * balance.
                                                                    (F)
C                    Return (H)  (   MiPrncpl * MiMnthlyInt )
C                              / (   1
C                                  - ( 1 + MiMnthlyInt ) ** -MiNoPmts )

P MnthlyPmt        E                                                (G)
```

Contrast the code at **B** and **C** in Figure 3.3 with that at **C** and **D** in Figure 3.2B. In Figure 3.3, I pass the three required parameters directly instead of using three Z-Add instructions. The simulated output parameter in Figure 3.2B (SuPmt) is now simply a value returned to the caller. We'll see exactly how this works in a moment.

One new element in program IntProc is the *prototype definition* for subprocedure MnthlyPmt, shown at **A** in Figure 3.3. The prototype definition defines the call interface between the program and the subprocedure. Notice that the definition is built entirely of RPG D-specs. The Source Entry Utility (SEU) line command for prompting these specifications is PD — just as it is for any D-spec.

The first line of the prototype contains the name of the subprocedure, MnthlyPmt, with a declaration type of PR (for prototype). The keyword Like(AuPmt) defines the return value for this procedure. I could have hard coded the type and length of the return value using the Length, Type, and Decimal position fields of the D-spec. Instead, I chose to specify that this procedure returns the same type and length as the screen field AuPmt — that is, a numeric value with a length of 11 and two decimal places.

After the PR statement at **A** are three D-specs that define the three parameters passed to the subprocedure. The RPG compiler assumes that D-specs that immediately follow a prototype declaration (PR) and have a blank declaration type are parameter definitions. Upon finding a D-spec with a nonblank declaration type or a specification other than a named constant (or a C declaration type D specification), the compiler ends parameter definitions for the procedure. This is exactly how the compiler determines which subfields are associated with a data structure. In this case, I define three parameters (MiPrncpl, MiYrInt, and MiNoPmts) to be passed to subprocedure MnthlyPmt. I again use the Like keyword in all three cases rather than hard coding the parameter types and lengths.

The three parameter definitions are formal definitions. As you can see at **B** and **C** in Figure 3.3, you don't have to use the names MiPrincpl, MiYrInt, and MiNoPmts. The only restriction is that the three parameters passed to the subprocedure must agree with these three in type and length. In fact, the parameter names MiPrincpl, MiYrInt, and MiNoPmts aren't even required in the parameter definition. I could have left the parameter names blank at **A**. However, I always use the names (even though the compiler ignores them) for documentation purposes.

Let's revisit **B** and **C** in the figure. Notice the procedure is invoked as if it were a numeric type. In fact, it is! As we've seen, it's defined to have a type and length Like(AuPmt) at **A** in the figure. Also, notice I pass three parameters separated by colons. These parameters must and do correspond in type and length to the three formal parameters defined at **A** in the prototype definition.

Because you're permitted to assign a type and length to an RPG subprocedure, you can use a procedure in any expression involving the extended Factor 2. For example, if Proc is a subprocedure whose type is packed 7,0 (seven digits with zero decimals), you can code something like the following:

```
C                    If        Proc( x ) + 1 > Proc( y )
```

The value of this method for improving program comprehension cannot be overstated. Suppose I have a subprocedure called AdjustedIncome that accepts an employee number as a parameter and returns that employee's adjusted income. Suppose further that I have a subprocedure called FedTax that calculates the employee's federal tax based on his or her adjusted income. Then I can code the following statement.[2]

```
C                      Eval        EmpFedTax
C                                  = FedTax( AdjustedIncome( EmpNo ) )
```

Such self-documenting code speeds program comprehension, which lowers the cost of program maintenance. In addition, because subprocedures are defined in the D-specs and invoked using the extended Factor 2, their names aren't restricted to 14 characters, as are RPG subroutines.

Note

Sometimes it's not appropriate to assign a type and length to an RPG subprocedure. In such cases, you invoke the subprocedure using the CallP (Call a Prototyped Procedure or Program) instruction. For example, if NoType is the name of a procedure that takes three parameters and doesn't have a type and length, you call it as follows:

```
C                      CallP       NoType( Parm1: Parm2: Parm3 )
```

Now let's look at subprocedure MnthlyPmt. MnthlyPmt is "sandwiched" between procedure begin (declaration type B) and procedure end (declaration type E) statements at **D** and **G**, respectively. These statements perform much the same functions that BegSr and EndSr statements perform for RPG subroutines. Procedure begin and end statements can be prompted with the SEU line command PPR.

At **E** is the *procedure interface*, which is nearly identical to the prototype definition at **A**. However, the first statement at **E** uses the declaration type PI (for procedure interface) instead of PR (for prototype). The differences between prototype definitions and procedure interfaces are:

- Prototypes begin with a statement that specifies the PR declaration type, whereas procedure interfaces use PI.

- The name of the procedure is required in the PR statement but is optional in the PI statement.

- The parameter names are optional in the prototype definition, but they're required in the procedure interface because they're the actual field declarations upon which the procedure will operate.

---

2 Actually, for this Eval statement to work, the FedTax procedure must pass its parameter by value or read-only reference. I explain passing parameters this way later in this chapter.

Finally, notice the Return statement at **F.** When coded in a subprocedure, a Return statement can contain (among other things) an expression. In this case, the expression is the value that procedure MnthlyPmt returns. In other words, the value placed in AuPmt and MoPmt at **B** and **C**, respectively, is this returned value.

In OPM, the RPG III RETRN instruction exits the program. In ILE RPG, Return exits the procedure. Naturally, if you're in the main procedure of a program — the portion of the program that precedes the first subprocedure — Return will exit the program. But if you're in an RPG subprocedure (as is the case here), the Return instruction simply takes you back to the instruction following the instruction that invoked the procedure.

All D-specs defined within a subprocedure (other than parameters) are local. For example, MiMnthlyInt (defined just after **E**) is local to subprocedure MnthlyPmt. This means MiMnthlyInt is available for use only within this subprocedure. Even if you defined another field with the same name elsewhere, it would be a different field. It could even have a different type and length.

Another thing to understand is that data items defined within procedures are *automatic* variables by default. This means they're created when the procedure is invoked and they're deleted when the procedure ends. Each time procedure MnthlyPmt is invoked, MiMnthlyInt is reallocated and reinitialized. If I need a variable to remain unmodified across procedure invocations, I must use the keyword Static as follows:

```
D MiMnthlyInt      S              8F    Static
```

The Static keyword places the variable in static storage, so it isn't initialized each time the procedure is invoked and instead retains the same value it had when the procedure previously ended.

In contrast, any data defined in the main procedure is global and static. If I'd defined MiMnthlyInt just after **A** instead of within the MnthlyPmt procedure, it would have been available in the main procedure and in all subprocedures of the program because data defined in the main procedure is global. Also, MiMnthlyInt would have been static. This means that if I'd defined MiMnthlyInt in the main procedure, it would have been allocated and initialized when the module was activated and deallocated when the module was deactivated. (Remember, the main procedure is all code — including F-, D-, I-, C-, and O-specs — that precedes the first subprocedure.)

Invoking Procedures in Other Modules

An ILE RPG program can't invoke a subprocedure in another program. However, it can invoke a subprocedure in a different module in the same program or invoke a subprocedure in a service program. I'll show you how to do this for modules bound by copy within an ILE program (although, in most instances, I don't believe it's useful to use bind by copy). The situation for service programs is similar. However, there are additional considerations, which I discuss in Chapter 4.

Figures 3.4A and 3.4B are actually the program of Figure 3.3 split into two modules.

FIGURE 3.4A

ILE RPG Module IntProcE

```
FIntD        CF    E              WorkStn

 * Prototype
D MnthlyPmt        PR              Like( AuPmt )
D  MiPrncpl                        Like( AuPrncpl )
D  MiYrInt                         Like( AuYrInt  )
D  MiNoPmts                        Like( AuNoPmts )


 * Loop until user presses the F3 key
C                 DoU       *IN03 = *On

C                 ExFmt     R01

C                 If        *IN03 = *On
C                 Leave
C                 EndIf

C                 If            AuPrncpl > *Zero
C                 And  AuYrInt  > *Zero
C                 And  AuNoPmts > *Zero

C                 Eval      AuPmt = MnthlyPmt( AuPrncpl:
C                                              AuYrInt:
C                                              AuNoPmts )

C                 Else
C                 Z-Add     *Zero          AuPmt

C                 EndIf

C                 If            MoPrncpl > *Zero
C                 And  MoYrInt  > *Zero
C                 And  MoNoPmts > *Zero

C                 Eval      MoPmt = MnthlyPmt( MoPrncpl:
C                                              MoYrInt:
C                                              MoNoPmts )

C                 Else
C                 Z-Add     *Zero          MoPmt

C                 EndIf

C                 EndDo

C                 Eval      *INLR = *On
```

FIGURE 3.4B
ILE RPG Module MnthlyPmt

```
Ⓐ  H NoMain

Ⓑ  FIntD      CF    E              WorkStn

    * Prototype
    D MnthlyPmt          PR                    Like( AuPmt )
    D   MiPrncpl                               Like( AuPrncpl )
    D   MiYrInt                                Like( AuYrInt )
    D   MiNoPmts                               Like( AuNoPmts )


    * = * = * = * = * = * = * = * = * = * = * = * = * = * = * = * = * =
    * MnthlyPmt procedure  - Calculate a monthly payment given
    *                        principal, interest, and number of
    *                        equal monthly payments
Ⓒ  P MnthlyPmt          B                     Export

    D MnthlyPmt          PI                    Like( AuPmt )
    D   MiPrncpl                               Like( AuPrncpl )
    D   MiYrInt                                Like( AuYrInt )
    D   MiNoPmts                               Like( AuNoPmts )

    * Local variables
    D MiMnthlyInt        S             8F


    * Calculate the fractional value for monthly interest
    * = to the yearly interest percent divided by 1200 (1200 = 12 months
    * times 100 percent)
    C                    Eval      MiMnthlyInt = MiYrInt / 1200

    * Use the formula m = (pi/(1 - (1 + i)**-n) to compute the
    * monthly interest. Note this computes an equal monthly
    * payment for an interest amount applied to a declining
    * balance.

    C                    Return (H)   (   MiPrncpl * MiMnthlyInt )
    C                              / (   1
    C                                  - ( 1 + MiMnthlyInt ) ** -MiNoPmts )

    * Following statement included to satisfy compiler. It
    * is never executed.
Ⓓ  C                    ExFmt     R01

    P MnthlyPmt          E
```

Figure 3.4A shows module IntProcE, which is no more than the main procedure of IntProc in Figure 3.3. The prototype for subprocedure MnthlyPmt is still required even though the subprocedure isn't in this module.

Tip

As you develop more and more subprocedures, you'll need to manage a large number of prototypes (one for each procedure). It's best to save these prototypes in source members and use RPG's /Copy compiler directive to copy the prototype from the RPG member containing the prototype.

Now look at the second module, which I called MnthlyPmt (Figure 3.4B). At **A** is a control specification specifying the NoMain keyword. This means there are no executable C-specs in the main module. Specifying NoMain doesn't preclude you from specifying D- and/or F-specs in the main procedure. Nor does it preclude you from coding non-executable C-specs, such as those that use the KLIST and DEFINE opcodes.

At **B**, I specified an F-spec for the display file. I did this solely to use the Like keyword with arguments specifying fields in this display file (such as in the prototype definition). An externally described data structure doesn't work for this purpose because it defines only input-capable fields (i.e., those specified with usage I or B in the DDS). Also, because I used an F-spec for a display file, I had to insert an ExFmt (Execute Format) statement at **D**. This statement will never be executed because it is preceded by a Return instruction.

The only other difference between the subprocedure as coded here and the subprocedure as coded in Figure 3.3 is the procedure begin statement at **C** in Figure 3.4B. Notice I've added the Export keyword. This simple addition makes procedure MnthlyPmt available to any module in the program. It doesn't, however, make the procedure available outside the program. Only service programs (which are covered in Chapter 4) can make procedures available outside themselves.

Passing Parameters to Subprocedures

Let's delve under the covers a bit to gain a better understanding of how parameters are passed to subprocedures. IBM doesn't publish the exact interface for passing parameters, but we can understand the situation conceptually without the specifics.

There are three ways to pass parameters to a subprocedure in ILE RPG: by reference, by value, and by read-only reference. The default is to pass parameters by reference.

Passing by Reference

How does the system pass parameters by reference? Again, IBM doesn't make this information explicit. Thus, the following description is conceptual only and isn't necessarily accurate with respect to the actual implementation of parameter passing on the AS/400. RPG allocates contiguous memory (referred to as the *parameter stack*) to contain parameter information. Suppose I have a subprocedure called Proc whose prototype looks like Figure 3.5.

FIGURE 3.5

Prototype for Subprocedure Proc When
Passing All Parameters by Reference

```
D Proc                    PR
D   Parm1                               10
D   Parm2                               5
D   Parm3                               7P 0
```

If field A is 10 characters, B is five characters, and C is a packed 7,0 field, I could invoke Proc as follows:

```
C                 CallP      Proc( A: B: C )
```

During processing of this CallP statement, the system must set up the parameter stack. The system sets three pointers to point to A, B, and C, respectively, in the parameter stack. Pointers on the AS/400 are 16 bytes in length. So the parameter stack might look something like that of Figure 3.6 when passing A, B, and C by reference.

FIGURE 3.6

Parameter Stack Used for Passing
A, B, and C by Reference

Position 01 to Position 16 = Pointer to A
Position 17 to Position 32 = Pointer to B
Position 33 to Position 48 = Pointer to C

Because we're passing pointers to the actual data, when the subprocedure changes any of these three parameters, the calling routine will "see" the changes. This should be familiar behavior because it's what happens when you pass parameters with a standard dynamic call using the Call opcode. (It's also what happens whenever you pass parameters with the CallB, or Call a Bound Procedure, opcode.)

The main drawback to passing parameters by reference is that we can't pass expressions. For example, the following statement would be invalid when passing parameters by reference:

```
C                 CallP      Proc( A + 'XYZ': B + 'ABC': C / 20 )
```

Because we're actually passing pointers to fields and the subprocedure can potentially modify those fields, expressions such as this aren't permitted when passing parameters by reference. However, they are permitted when passing parameters by value.

Passing by Value
Consider the prototype of Figure 3.7.

FIGURE 3.7

*Prototype for Subprocedure Proc When
Passing One Parameter by Value*

```
D Proc            PR
D   Parm1                         1Ø
D   Parm2                          5     Value
D   Parm3                         7P Ø
```

This time the second parameter definition uses the Value keyword, which tells the compiler to pass the second parameter by value. Because the first and third parameters have no keywords, they'll default to being passed by reference. (RPG has no explicit Reference keyword).

To understand what it means to pass parameters by value, assume that field B currently contains the character string 'RPGIV' and consider the same call we used before:

```
C                 CallP    Proc( A: B: C )
```

This time, because B is being passed by value, the parameter stack will be different. Figure 3.8 gives you an idea of what the parameter stack looks like.

FIGURE 3.8

*Parameter Stack Used for Passing
A and C by Reference and B by Value*

Position 01 to Position 16 = Pointer to A
Position 17 to Position 21 = 'RPGIV'
Position 33 to Position 48 = Pointer to C

Notice positions 17–21 now contain the actual value of parameter B rather than a pointer to B. Because the parameter stack contains only a copy of the original value, changes made to this parameter are made directly to the parameter stack and therefore aren't "seen" by the invoking procedure. Also, I can pass a value parameter as an expression. For example, suppose D is a three-character string containing the value 'RPG' and E is a two-character string containing 'IV'. The following CallP statement results in a parameter stack like that of Figure 3.8:

```
C                 CallP    Proc( A: D + E: C )
```

When you pass parameters by value, RPG relaxes many of the constraints on matching parameters to the prototype by type and length. For example, suppose a parameter passed by value is defined as a packed 11,2 field. You could then pass this parameter as a zoned 7,3 field or a packed 9,2 field. You could even pass a 13,2 field, as long as the value doesn't overflow the defined number of digits to the left of the decimal point.

The basic rules for a parameter passed by value are

- If the value parameter is defined as numeric, the field or expression passed must also be numeric.
- If the value parameter is defined as character or graphic, the field or expression passed by value must also be character or graphic.
- If you pass a character or graphic field or expression using a value that's longer than the defined length of the parameter, the system truncates the field to the defined length. If the character or graphic value passed is shorter than the defined length, the system adds blank characters to reach the defined length.
- If you pass a numeric field or expression with more decimal positions than are defined for the value parameter, the system truncates the excess decimal values (those appearing to the right of the defined number of decimal positions).
- A numeric field or expression being passed by value must not have more significant digits to the left of the decimal point than the parameter can accommodate. To understand this rule, suppose I have a value parameter defined as 2,0. I can pass any value between –99 and +99 for this parameter. Any value passed for such a parameter that falls outside this range will result in a runtime error.

If you think about all this, you should understand why a procedure that's expecting to receive a parameter by value would fail if it actually received the parameter by reference. The reverse is also true; a procedure expecting a parameter to be passed by reference would fail if it received the parameter by value.

Also, if a procedure modifies a parameter passed by value, the invoking procedure won't see the modification because the parameter is placed directly in the parameter stack, to which the invoking procedure has no direct access.

You probably wouldn't want to pass a large parameter by value. For example, if you pass a 32,000-entry array by value and each array entry is 100 bytes large, the system must allocate 3.2 million bytes of memory in the parameter stack for this purpose. Worse yet, this allocation is repeated for each concurrent user of your program. Such inefficient use of memory often leads to high nondatabase faulting, which causes performance problems. Later in this chapter, I provide more details about which of the three passing methods to choose.

Using Expressions in Parameters: A Closer Look

In case you're having trouble imagining cases where you might want to use expressions in parameters, consider the example depicted in Figures 3.9A, 3.9B, and 3.9C (pages 37 and 38).

FIGURE 3.9A

IntTbl Setup Screen Before Input

```
 6/03/00                    Interest Table Setup              S100B54R
 08:42:02                                                     MCRAVITZ



    Principal:              _____

    Starting Interest:         _____        e.g., 7.5 means 7.5%

    Total Number
    of Payments:               ___


           F3=Exit
```

FIGURE 3.9B

IntTbl Setup Screen with Input

```
 6/03/00                    Interest Table Setup              S100B54R
 08:42:02                                                     MCRAVITZ



    Principal:          100000_____

    Starting Interest:         6_____       e.g., 7.5 means 7.5%

    Total Number
    of Payments:              360_


           F3=Exit
```

ILE RPG program IntTbl lets a user enter a principal, starting interest rate, and number of payments and displays four possible monthly payments for various interest rates, starting at the specified rate. In Figure 3.9B, we request information for a $100,000 loan financed over 30 years (360 months) at a starting interest rate of 6 percent. Figure 3.9C shows the outcome. It shows that a 6 percent loan would produce a monthly payment of $599.55. A 6.5 percent loan (6 percent plus 0.5 percent) would produce a monthly payment of $632.07. A 7 percent loan (6 percent plus 1 percent) would produce a monthly payment of $665.30. Finally, a 7.5 percent loan (6 percent plus 1.5 percent) would produce a monthly payment of $699.21.

Figure 3.9C
IntTbl Interest Screen

```
┌─────────────────────────────────────────────────────────────────────┐
│    6/03/00                     Interest Table              S100B54R   │
│    08:49:48                                                MCRAVITZ   │
│                                                                       │
│                                                                       │
│       Principal:              100,000.00                              │
│       Number of Payments:        360                                  │
│                                                                       │
│    Monthly Payments For...                                            │
│                                                                       │
│        6.00 Pct           Plus .5%          Plus 1%        Plus 1.5%  │
│                                                                       │
│         599.55             632.07            665.30         699.21    │
│                                                                       │
│       Press Enter to Continue                                         │
│                                                                       │
└─────────────────────────────────────────────────────────────────────┘
```

Figures 3.10A, 3.10B, and 3.10C show the code for this interest-calculating application.

Figure 3.10A
Display File IntTblD

```
A                              DSPSIZ(24 80 *DS3)
A         R R01
A                              CA03(03)
A                         1  3DATE
A                              EDTCDE(Y)

A                              COLOR(WHT)
A                         2  3TIME
A                              COLOR(WHT)
A                         1 31'Interest Table Setup'
A                              COLOR(WHT)
A                         1 69SYSNAME
A                              COLOR(WHT)
A                         2 69USER
A                              COLOR(WHT)
A                         7  6'Principal:'
A         PRNCPL   11Y 2I   7 25COMP(GT 0.00)
A                         9  6'Starting Interest:'
A         STRINT    5Y 2I   9 31COMP(GT 0.00)
A                         9 41'e.g., 7.5 means 7.5%'
A                        11  6'Total Number'
A                        12  6'of Payments:'
A         NOPMTS    3S 0I  12 31
A                        15 15'F3=Exit'
A                              COLOR(BLU)
```

continued

FIGURE 3.10A *CONTINUED*

```
A               R R02
A                                        1  3DATE
A                                           EDTCDE(Y)
A                                           COLOR(WHT)
A                                        2  3TIME
A                                           COLOR(WHT)
A                                        1 34'Interest Table'
A                                           COLOR(WHT)
A                                        1 69SYSNAME
A                                           COLOR(WHT)
A                                        2 69USER
A                                           COLOR(WHT)
A                                        7  6'Principal:'
A                                           COLOR(WHT)
A               PRNCPL     11Y 20       7 25EDTCDE(1)
A                                           COLOR(WHT)
A                                        8  6'Number of Payments:'
A                                           COLOR(WHT)
A               NOPMTS      3Y 00       8 33EDTCDE(1)
A                                           COLOR(WHT)
A                                       11  4'Monthly Payments For...'
A                                           COLOR(WHT)
A                                       18 10'Press Enter to Continue'
A                                           COLOR(BLU)
A               STRINT      5Y 20      13  9EDTCDE(1)
A                                           COLOR(WHT)
A                                       13 16'Pct'
A                                           COLOR(WHT)
A               PMT1       11Y 20      15  5EDTCDE(1)
A               PMT2       11Y 20      15 23EDTCDE(1)
A                                       13 48'Plus 1%'
A                                           COLOR(WHT)
A               PMT3       11Y 20      15 41EDTCDE(1)
A                                       13 29'Plus .5%'
A                                           COLOR(WHT)
A               PMT4       11Y 20      15 58EDTCDE(1)
A                                       13 63'Plus 1.5%'
A                                           COLOR(WHT)
```

FIGURE 3.10B
ILE RPG Module IntTbl

```
FIntTblD   CF   E            WorkStn

 * Prototype(s)
D MnthlyPmt      PR              Like( Pmt1    )
D  MiPrncpl                      Like( Prncpl ) Value
D  MiYrInt                       Like( StrInt ) Value
D  MiNoPmts                      Like( NoPmts ) Value

 * Loop until user presses F3
C                  DoU     *IN03 = *On
```

continued

FIGURE **3.10B** CONTINUED

```
C                       ExFmt      RØ1

C                       If         *INØ3 = *On
C                       Leave
C                       EndIf

   * Calculate the payments
 A C                    Eval       Pmt1 = MnthlyPmt( Prncpl: StrInt + Ø.Ø:
   C                                                 NoPmts )
   C                    Eval       Pmt2 = MnthlyPmt( Prncpl: StrInt + Ø.5:
   C                                                 NoPmts )
   C                    Eval       Pmt3 = MnthlyPmt( Prncpl: StrInt + 1.Ø:
   C                                                 NoPmts )
   C                    Eval       Pmt4 = MnthlyPmt( Prncpl: StrInt + 1.5:
   C                                                 NoPmts )

   C                    ExFmt      RØ2

   C                    EndDo

   C                    Eval       *INLR = *On
```

FIGURE **3.10C**

Excerpt from ILE RPG Module MnthlyPmt1

```
     .
     .
     .
   * Prototype
 D MnthlyPmt     PR                Like( Pmt1     )
 D  MiPrncpl                       Like( Prncpl   ) Value
 D  MiYrInt                        Like( StrInt   ) Value
 D  MiNoPmts                       Like( NoPmts   ) Value
     .
     .
     .
   * = * = * = * = * = * = * = * = * = * = * = * = * = * = * = * = * =
   * MnthlyPmt procedure -  Calculate a monthly payment given
   *                        principal, interest, and number of
   *                        equal monthly payments
 P MnthlyPmt     B                 Export

 D MnthlyPmt     PI                Like( Pmt1     )
 D  MiPrncpl                       Like( Prncpl   ) Value
 D  MiYrInt                        Like( StrInt   ) Value
 D  MiNoPmts                       Like( NoPmts   ) Value
     .
     .
     .
```

This program uses the MnthlyPmt procedure in module MnthlyPmt1, which has been modified to receive three parameters by value. There's virtually no difference between module MnthlyPmt1 in Figure 3.10C and module MnthlyPmt in Figure 3.4B except for the use of the Value keywords in the prototype and procedure interface in module MnthlyPmt1.

The advantage of passing a parameter by value is shown at **A** in Figure 3.10B. Notice how expressions simplify and clarify the code. By contrast, look at Figure 3.11 to see how we would have written this same code fragment had we passed the parameters by reference.

FIGURE 3.11

Invoking the MnthlyPmt Procedure When Passing by Reference

```
              .
              .
              .
C                    Eval      WrkFld = StrInt + 0.0                          (A)
C                    Eval      Pmt1 = MnthlyPmt( Prncpl: WrkFld:
C                                        NoPmts )
C                    Eval      WrkFld = StrInt + 0.5                          (B)
C                    Eval      Pmt2 = MnthlyPmt( Prncpl: WrkFld:
C                                        NoPmts )
C                    Eval      WrkFld = StrInt + 1.0                          (C)
C                    Eval      Pmt3 = MnthlyPmt( Prncpl: WrkFld:
C                                        NoPmts )
C                    Eval      WrkFld = StrInt + 1.5                          (D)
C                    Eval      Pmt4 = MnthlyPmt( Prncpl: WrkFld:
C                                        NoPmts )
              .
              .
              .
```

The fact that we have to set the second parameter (at **A**, **B**, **C**, and **D**) before invoking the procedure obscures what's really happening here.

Passing by Read-Only Reference

The third way to pass parameters is by read-only reference. Passing parameters by read-only reference is first and foremost passing parameters by reference. This means that the address (not the value) of the parameter is placed in the parameter stack. The difference with read-only reference is that the subprocedure promises to the compiler that it won't modify the parameter. The compiler enforces this promise only if the subprocedure is contained in the module being compiled. In other words, if the subprocedure was contained in a different module, it could define the parameter to be passed by ordinary reference and the compiler would have no way to check it.

To pass parameters by read-only reference, you code the Const keyword. Figure 3.12 shows an example of a prototype in which Parm2 is passed by read-only reference.

FIGURE 3.12
*Prototype for Subprocedure Proc When
Passing One Parameter by Read-Only Reference*

```
D Proc            PR
D   Parm1                    10
D   Parm2                     5    Const
D   Parm3                    7P 0
```

As when you pass parameters by value, you may pass expressions when you pass parameters by read-only reference. (I include in the term *expression* parameters whose size is different from the size defined in the prototype.) If you pass an expression for a parameter that's defined as read-only reference, the system evaluates the expression and then allocates memory to hold its result. It then places a pointer to the allocated memory location into the parameter stack. Thus, the parameter is passed by reference. The read-only aspect is a promise to the compiler that the parameter is unmodified by the subprocedure. As I explained, the compiler checks this promise only when the subprocedure resides in the same source as the invoking procedure. Otherwise, the read-only aspects are checked only if the prototype in the module containing the subprocedure specifies the Const keyword for the parameter.

Choosing Whether to Pass Parameters by Reference, by Value, or by Read-Only Reference

Now that you've learned the three ways to pass parameters, which do you choose? In the summary in Figure 3.13, I first attempt an answer in a pure ILE environment. (By *pure ILE environment*, I mean invoking an RPG subprocedure from an ILE RPG program.) I discuss special considerations regarding invoking OPM programs in the next section.

FIGURE 3.13
How to Pass Parameters in a Pure ILE Environment

Reference	Value	Read-only reference	Parameter modified by subprocedure	Requirement to pass parameter as expression	Parameter is larger than 100 bytes
X			Yes	n/a	n/a
	X		No	Yes	No
	X		No	Yes	Yes
	X		No	No	No
		X	No	No	Yes

I advocate passing either by value or by read-only reference (unless there's a requirement to modify the parameter) because these methods let you pass an expression. Even in cases where you don't need to pass an expression, passing by value or by read-only reference leaves open the possibility of passing an expression in the future.

In most instances where there's no requirement for the subprocedure to modify the parameter, you should pass the parameter by value. In addition to giving a programmer the flexibility to pass expressions, passing by value also tells the programmer that the parameter isn't modified by the subprocedure. A parameter passed by value can be modified, but the modification isn't seen by the invoking procedure.

Note

Some languages, such as CL, pass parameters only by reference, and any procedures passing parameters by value will be unavailable for direct use by such languages. This is an important design consideration and represents one case where you might choose to pass parameters by reference.

It's usually more convenient to pass a parameter by value than by read-only reference, but in one case, passing by read-only reference uses less memory. When the read-only reference parameter is simply the name of a field and matches the type and length specified in the prototype for the parameter, the system places a 16-byte pointer to the parameter without allocating additional memory to hold the parameter itself. When you pass by value, the system always must allocate memory (in the call stack) to hold the value of the parameter.

Passing parameters by value is usually more convenient than passing by read-only reference because the compiler lets you modify a value parameter within a subprocedure but not a read-only reference parameter. Of course, the calling procedure won't have access to the modification. However, the compiler is so fastidious about not letting you modify a read-only reference parameter that it won't let you pass it as a parameter if there's even a possibility it can be modified. Figure 3.14 shows (at **A**) some sample code that would be flagged with a severity-30 compile error, "RNF5035 Result field must be a field that can be modified."

FIGURE 3.14

RPG Module That Would Cause an RNF5035 Compile Error

```
D Proc            PR
D   Parm1                         1    Const

C                 CallP     Proc( 'A' )
C                 Eval      *INLR = *On

P Proc            B

D Proc            PI
D   Parm1                         1    Const

C                 Call      'PGM'
C                 Parm                    Parm1                    (A)

C                 Return

P Proc            E
```

This subprocedure could be compiled successfully if I'd specified that I wanted to receive Parm1 by value instead of by read-only reference.

Prototyping Program Calls

ILE RPG lets you prototype calls to OPM programs, which lets you pass expressions for those parameters that aren't modified by the OPM program. You can take advantage of this capability with your in-house OPM programs, but it's particularly useful when you're invoking OPM APIs.

One commonly used API is QCMDEXC (Execute Command), which you can invoke from any high-level language (HLL) to execute AS/400 commands. QCMDEXC is passed two parameters: the first is a character string containing an AS/400 command; the second is a packed 15,5 numeric field specifying the length of the first parameter. (A third, optional parameter lets you specify whether you want to pass Double-Byte Character Set data.) Figure 3.15 shows sample code that invokes QCMDEXC via a prototyped call.

FIGURE 3.15

ILE RPG Program WrkUsr

```
(A)   *Prototype for QCMDEXC
      D As400Cmd        PR                        ExtPgm( 'QCMDEXC' )
      D   Cmd                          200        Const
      D                                           Options( *VarSize )
      D   Len                         15P 5 Const

      D WrkUsrJob       C                         'WrkUsrJob'

      D UserId          S              10

      C       *Entry        Plist
      C                     Parm                       UserId

(B)   C                     CallP     As400Cmd( WrkUsrJob            +
      C                                         ' '                  +
      C                                         UserId:
      C                                         %Size( WrkUsrJob )   +
      C                                         1                    +
      C                                         %Size( UserId ) )

      C                     Eval      *INLR = *On
```

Although QCMDEXC is more typically used to invoke one of the AS/400 override commands, I've used it to invoke the WrkUsrJob (Work with User Jobs) command as a change of pace. Look at the prototype at **A** in Figure 3.15. When prototyping an OPM function, you must use the ExtPgm keyword with the PR statement as shown. The prototype name (As400Cmd) will be the name used for QCMDEXC in the program. I use the Const keyword for both parameters to signal that they're being passed by read-only reference. This lets me use expressions for them. Also, I couldn't have passed these parameters by value because OPM programs always receive parameters by reference. Specifying Options(*VarSize) for parameter Cmd instructs the compiler to pass the actual length of the parameter up to a maximum of the specified length (in this case, 200 bytes). In other words, the length of 200 specified for this parameter is treated as a maximum size and not the actual size of the parameter.

Now look at the call to QCMDEXC at **B**. Notice how I'm able to take advantage of the fact that I can pass parameters as expressions. Anybody who's coded calls to QCMDEXC in RPG should appreciate how much easier this is versus how it must be done in RPG/400. Remember: Although this illustration shows how to prototype a call to QCMDEXC, you can use this technique to call any OPM program, including legacy RPG/400 programs. Moreover, although I've confined my discussion to OPM programs, you can use this same technique to prototype calls to ILE programs, too.

Suppressing Parameters

At times, it can be handy to suppress parameters when you're invoking a subprocedure. ILE RPG supports two methods of parameter suppression: Options(*Omit) and Options(*NoPass). Let's discuss Options(*Omit) first.

*Options (*Omit)*

You can use Options(*Omit) to assign default values to parameters when you can't predict a particular pattern of suppression. To see what I mean, let's return to the interest calculation application we discussed earlier in this chapter. Suppose I want to assign default values of $100,000 to the principal, 7 percent to the interest, and 360 months to the number of payments. In other words, wherever the user has placed a value of 0 on the screen, I want to use the corresponding default value.

Figure 3.16A shows an interest calculation screen where the user has filled in all three input values with nonzero amounts. In this case, the program simply calculates the monthly payment as before. But Figure 3.16B shows a situation where the user has placed zero values for yearly interest and the number of monthly payments. In this case, the program uses the default values (7 percent and 360) to calculate the monthly payment.

FIGURE 3.16A

Interest Calculation Screen Without Default Values

```
 6/30/00                  Personal Planner                    MCRAVITZ
 08:46:35                                                      S100B54R


    Amount Financed:              90,000.00    0 Defaults to 100,000.00
    Yearly Interest:                   6.50    0 Defaults to 7 percent
    Number of Equal
    Monthly Payments:                 360      0 Defaults to 360 Months

       Loan Monthly Payment---------------------       568.86


          F3=Exit
```

FIGURE 3.16B

Interest Calculation Screen with Default Values

```
 6/30/00                  Personal Planner                    MCRAVITZ
 08:46:35                                                      S100B54R


    Amount Financed:              90,000.00    0 Defaults to 100,000.00
    Yearly Interest:                    .00    0 Defaults to 7 percent
    Number of Equal
    Monthly Payments:                  0       0 Defaults to 360 Months

       Loan Monthly Payment---------------------       598.77


          F3=Exit
```

Figure 3.17A shows the IntDO display file DDS used in this program. Figure 3.17B shows the IntProcO RPG program.

FIGURE 3.17A

Display File IntDO

```
A                                     DSPSIZ(24 80 *DS3)
A            R R01
A                                     CA03(03)
A                          1   3DATE
A                                     EDTCDE(Y)
A                                     COLOR(WHT)
A                          1 69USER
A                                     COLOR(WHT)
```

continued

FIGURE 3.17A *Continued*

```
A                                2  3TIME
A                                   COLOR(WHT)
A                                2 69SYSNAME
A                                   COLOR(WHT)
A                                1 33'Personal Planner'
A                                   COLOR(WHT)
A                                6  4'Amount Financed:'
A          AUPRNCPL   11Y 2B     6 31EDTCDE(J)
A                                   COMP(GE .00)
A                                7  4'Yearly Interest:'
A          AUYRINT     5Y 2B     7 39EDTCDE(J)
A                                   COMP(GE .00)
A                                8  4'Number of Equal'
A                                9  4'Monthly Payments:'
A          AUNOPMTS    3Y 0B     9 39EDTCDE(J)
A                                   COMP(GE 0)
A                               11  6'Loan Monthly Payment----------------
A                                   -------'
A          AUPMT      11Y 20    11 48EDTCDE(J)
A                                   COLOR(BLU)
A                                6 51'0 Defaults to 100,000.00'
A                                   COLOR(RED)
A                                7 51'0 Defaults to 7 percent'
A                                   COLOR(RED)
A                                9 51'0 Defaults to 360 Months'
A                                   COLOR(RED)
A                               14 10'F3=Exit'
A                                   COLOR(BLU)
```

FIGURE 3.17B

ILE RPG Program IntProcO

```
FIntDO     CF   E           WorkStn

 * Prototype
D MnthlyPmt        PR              Like( AuPmt )          (A)
D  MiPrncpl                        Like(    AuPrncpl )
D                                  Options( *Omit    )
D  MiYrInt                         Like(    AuYrInt  )
D                                  Options( *Omit    )
D  MiNoPmts                        Like(    AuNoPmts )
D                                  Options( *Omit    )

 * Loop until user presses the F3 key
C                DoU     *IN03 = *On

C                ExFmt   R01

C                If      *IN03 = *On
C                Leave
C                EndIf
```

continued

FIGURE 3.17B CONTINUED

```
B   * Invoke the MnthlyPmt procedure using *Omit wherever the user
    * has specified a zero value on the screen
C                       Select

C                       When        AuPrncpl  = *Zero
C                       And AuYrInt   = *Zero
C                       And AuNoPmts  = *Zero
C                       Eval        AuPmt = MnthlyPmt( *Omit:
C                                                     *Omit:
C                                                     *Omit    )

C                       When        AuPrncpl  = *Zero
C                       And AuYrInt   = *Zero
C                       And AuNoPmts <> *Zero
C                       Eval        AuPmt = MnthlyPmt( *Omit:
C                                                     *Omit:
C                                                     AuNoPmts )

C                       When        AuPrncpl  = *Zero
C                       And AuYrInt  <> *Zero
C                       And AuNoPmts  = *Zero
C                       Eval        AuPmt = MnthlyPmt( *Omit:
C                                                     AuYrInt:
C                                                     *Omit    )

C                       When        AuPrncpl  = *Zero
C                       And AuYrInt  <> *Zero
C                       And AuNoPmts <> *Zero
C                       Eval        AuPmt = MnthlyPmt( *Omit:
C                                                     AuYrInt:
C                                                     AuNoPmts )

C                       When        AuPrncpl <> *Zero
C                       And AuYrInt   = *Zero
C                       And AuNoPmts  = *Zero
C                       Eval        AuPmt = MnthlyPmt( AuPrncpl:
C                                                     *Omit:
C                                                     *Omit    )

C                       When        AuPrncpl <> *Zero
C                       And AuYrInt   = *Zero
C                       And AuNoPmts <> *Zero
C                       Eval        AuPmt = MnthlyPmt( AuPrncpl:
C                                                     *Omit:
C                                                     AuNoPmts )

C                       When        AuPrncpl <> *Zero
C                       And AuYrInt  <> *Zero
C                       And AuNoPmts  = *Zero
C                       Eval        AuPmt = MnthlyPmt( AuPrncpl:
C                                                     AuYrInt:
C                                                     *Omit    )

C                       When        AuPrncpl <> *Zero
C                       And AuYrInt  <> *Zero
```

continued

FIGURE 3.17B *Continued*

```
C                           And AuNoPmts <> *Zero                              (B)
C                 Eval      AuPmt = MnthlyPmt( AuPrncpl:
C                                             AuYrInt:
C                                             AuNoPmts )

C                 EndSl

C                 EndDo

C                 Eval      *INLR = *On


* = * = * = * = * = * = * = * = * = * = * = * = * = * = * = * =
* MnthlyPmt procedure  - Calculate a monthly payment given
*                        principal, interest, and number of
*                        equal monthly payments
P MnthlyPmt      B

D MnthlyPmt      PI                  Like( AuPmt )
D  MiPrncpl                          Like(    AuPrncpl )
D                                    Options( *Omit    )
D  MiYrInt                           Like(    AuYrInt  )
D                                    Options( *Omit    )
D  MiNoPmts                          Like(    AuNoPmts )
D                                    Options( *Omit    )

* Local variables
D MiMnthlyInt    S             8F
D MiPrncplUsed   S                   Like(    AuPrncpl )              (C)
D                                    Inz(     100000   )
D MiYrIntUsed    S                   Like(    AuYrInt  )
D                                    Inz(     7        )
D MiNoPmtsUsed   S                   Like(    AuNoPmts )
D                                    Inz(     360      )

* For every *OMITted parameter, use its default value               (D)
* (which was set via the INZ keyword). Otherwise
* use the parameter value passed to this procedure.
* Note, a parameter is passed as *Omit if its address
* is equal to *Null.
C                 If        %Addr( MiPrncpl ) <> *Null
C                 Eval      MiPrncplUsed = MiPrncpl
C                 EndIf

C                 If        %Addr( MiYrInt ) <> *Null
C                 Eval      MiYrIntUsed = MiYrInt
C                 EndIf

C                 If        %Addr( MiNoPmts ) <> *Null
C                 Eval      MiNoPmtsUsed = MiNoPmts
C                 EndIf

* Calculate the fractional value for monthly interest
* = to the yearly interest percent divided by 1200 (1200 = 12 months
* times 100 percent)
C                 Eval      MiMnthlyInt = MiYrIntUsed / 1200
```

continued

FIGURE 3.17B *Continued*

```
* Use the formula m = (pi/(1 - (1 + i)**-n) to compute the
* monthly interest. Note this computes an equal monthly
* payment for an interest amount applied to a declining
* balance.

C                    Return (H)   (   MiPrncplUsed * MiMnthlyInt )
C                                / (   1
C                                - ( 1 + MiMnthlyInt ) ** -MiNoPmtsUsed )

P MnthlyPmt       E
```

At **A** in Figure 3.17B is the prototype for the MnthlyPmt procedure. The only difference between this prototype and the one at **A** in Figure 3.3 is that I've added the Options(*Omit) keyword to each of the three parameters. At **B,** I've coded a Select/EndSl block that invokes the MnthlyPmt procedure using the *Omit placeholder wherever the user has specified a value of zero on the screen. A parameter passed as *Omit tells the procedure to use the default value for that parameter. To see how I accomplish this, let's look at the MnthlyPmt procedure.

At **C,** I've defined three fields corresponding to the three parameters. In fact, I've given these three fields the same names as the corresponding parameters plus a suffix of "Used." I'll refer to these three fields as the *Used fields.* So MiPrncplUsed corresponds to the MiPrncpl parameter. If the user omits a parameter, the corresponding Used field will contain the default value; otherwise, the field will be modified to contain the value passed as a parameter.

Notice that the three Used fields at **C** all use Inz keywords to specify the default values. Earlier I explained that variables defined in procedures are automatic by default — meaning that they're reallocated each time the procedure is invoked and (more important for the current discussion) reinitialized each time the procedure is invoked. We can, therefore, assume that the three Used fields at **C** will always contain the correct default values each time the procedure is invoked.

At **D,** I change the default values to the parameter values in the event that the parameter values weren't omitted. The system places a *Null value (essentially 16 bytes of binary zeros) into the parameter stack wherever the user omits a parameter, so I test for an omitted parameter by determining whether its address is equal to *Null.

Note

You can't specify Options(*Omit) for a parameter passed by value because no pointers are involved in that case.

The rest of the calculations are the same as those in Figure 3.3 except that I've replaced parameters with their corresponding Used values.

Options(*Omit) can help you overcome one syntactical weakness in ILE RPG. Suppose I have a procedure that requires no parameters. I'm not allowed to designate that it accepts no parameters when invoking the procedure. For example, consider procedure Today of Figure 3.18.

FIGURE 3.18

Procedure Today

```
H NoMain
 * Prototypes
D Today           PR              29
D  Dummy                           1    Options( *Omit )

D DayOfWeek       PR               9
D  InpDate                         D

D DayOfWeekArr    S                9    Dim(   7 )
D                                       CtData
D                                       PerRcd( 7 )

D MonthArr        S                9    Dim(  12 )
D                                       CtData
D                                       PerRcd( 3 )


 * = * = * = * = * = * = * = * = * = * = * = * = * = * = * = * =
 * Procedure DayOfWeek - Returns a spelled-out day of week for a
 *                       particular input date

P DayOfWeek       B                     Export

D DayOfWeek       PI               9
D  InpDate                         D

 * Local variables
D AnySunday       S                D    Inz( D'1999-07-04' )
D ElpsdDays       S              11P 0
D Quotient        S              11P 0
D Remainder       S              11P 0

 * Calculate number of elapsed days from a fixed Sunday until
 * the input date
C       AnySunday    SubDur  InpDate       ElpsdDays:*D

 * Dividing number of elapsed days by 7 and taking the remainder
 * gives us a representation of the day of the week, where 0
 * is Sunday
C       ElpsdDays    Div     7              Quotient
C                    MvR                    Remainder

 * Because RPG will use a negative remainder, I need to make it
 * a non-negative number in that case
C                    If      Remainder < *Zero
C                    Eval    Remainder = Remainder + 7
C                    EndIf
```

continued

FIGURE 3.18 *CONTINUED*

```
* Must add 1 to the remainder because array indices are 1-origin
C                     Return    DayOfWeekArr( Remainder + 1 )

P DayOfWeek       E

* = * = * = * = * = * = * = * = * = * = * = * = * = * = * = * = * =
* Procedure Today - Returns a string spelling out the current date

P Today           B                     Export

D Today           PI           29
D   Dummy                        1      Options( *Omit )

  * Local variables
D MonthNum        S             2P 0
D DayNum          S             2P 0
D YearNum         S             4P 0
D TodaysDate      S              D

  * Pick up today's date. Extract month and year
C                     Time                    TodaysDate
C                     Extrct    TodaysDate:*M MonthNum
C                     Extrct    TodaysDate:*Y YearNum
C                     Extrct    TodaysDate:*D DayNum

  * Return spelled-out description of the date
C                     Return    %Trim( DayOfWeek( TodaysDate ) )
C                               + ', '
C                               + %Trim( MonthArr( MonthNum ) )
C                               + ' '
C                               + %Trim( %EditC( DayNum: '3' ) )
C                               + ', '
C                               + %Trim( %EditC( YearNum: '3' ) )

P Today           E
*
  * Compile-time data

**CtData DayOfWeekArr
Sunday    Monday    Tuesday  WednesdayThursday Friday    Saturday
**CtData MonthArr
January   February  March
April     May       June
July      August    September
October   November  December
```

Ⓐ

This subprocedure returns today's day of week and date spelled out. For example, on July 1, 1999, the procedure returns the string "Thursday, July 1, 1999". At **A**, I've specified a parameter called Dummy, which is never referenced anywhere in the subprocedure's C-specs, as Options(*Omit). A typical use of this procedure might look something like this:

```
C                     Eval      PrtLine = Today( *Omit )
C                     Write     PrtRec
```

Because the parameter is defined with the Options(*Omit) keyword, I can invoke the Today procedure as shown. This method makes it clear that Today is the name of a procedure and not the name of some other type of data item. Had I not specified the dummy parameter with Options(*Omit), I'd have to code the above statements as follows:

```
C                       Eval      PrtLine = Today
C                       Write     PrtRec
```

In this case, it would be hard for a maintenance programmer to quickly discern that Today is the name of a procedure. Naturally, the programmer can look at the D-specs to find this out, but doing so is laborious and error prone.

Options(*NoPass)

Our other choice for parameter suppression is Options (*NoPass). Options(*NoPass) means you're literally "not passing" the parameter. This differs from Options(*Omit), with which you actually pass a null pointer for the parameter.

To illustrate an effective use of Options(*NoPass), I use an excerpt of service program DtTmHdl, which consists of a single module (also called DtTmHdl). The procedures in the module let you perform date and time arithmetic in RPG's extended Factor 2. (RPG provides only opcodes AddDur and SubDur for performing date, time, and timestamp arithmetic, and these opcodes don't use the extended Factor 2.) The source for service program DtTmHdl includes a full description of how to install and use the program, but for our purposes, I've extracted into Figure 3.19 only the portion of the code pertaining to the AddDate procedure.

FIGURE 3.19

Subset of ILE RPG Program DtTmHdl Pertaining to the AddDate Procedure

```
H NoMain

 * Public prototypes                                               (A)
D AddDate         PR              D
D   InpDate                       D   Value
D   DurAmt                      11P 0 Value
D   DurCode                      10   Value
D   DurAmt2                     11P 0 Value Options( *NoPass )
D   DurCode2                     10   Value Options( *NoPass )
D   DurAmt3                     11P 0 Value Options( *NoPass )
D   DurCode3                     10   Value Options( *NoPass )
        .
        .
        .

 * Other data
D LoCase          C                   'abcdefghijklmnopqrstuvwxyz'
D UpCase          C                   'ABCDEFGHIJKLMNOPQRSTUVWXYZ'
```

continued

FIGURE 3.19 *Continued*

```
* = * = * = * = * = * = * = * = * = * = * = * = * = * = * = * = * =
* Procedure AddDate - Add 1, 2, or 3 different durations to a date

P AddDate        B                      Export

D AddDate        PI            D
D  InpDate                     D    Value
D  DurAmt                   11P 0  Value
D  DurCode                    10   Value
D  DurAmt2                  11P 0  Value Options( *NoPass )
D  DurCode2                   10   Value Options( *NoPass )
D  DurAmt3                  11P 0  Value Options( *NoPass )
D  DurCode3                   10   Value Options( *NoPass )

D Parms          S           5P 0

 * Four simulated parameters used by subroutine AddDurSubr
D SubrDate       S             D
D SubrDurCode    S            10
D SubrDurAmt     S          11P 0

 * Add in the required duration
C              Eval      SubrDate    = InpDate
C    LoCase:UpCase Xlate  DurCode       SubrDurCode
C              Eval      SubrDurAmt  = DurAmt
C              ExSr      AddDurSubr
```

(B)
```
 * Add in the optional durations (if any)
C              Eval      Parms = %Parms
```

(C)
```
C              If        Parms >= 5
C    LoCase:UpCase Xlate  DurCode2      SubrDurCode
C              Eval      SubrDurAmt  = DurAmt2
C              ExSr      AddDurSubr
C              EndIf
```

(D)
```
C              If        Parms >= 7
C    LoCase:UpCase Xlate  DurCode3      SubrDurCode
C              Eval      SubrDurAmt  = DurAmt3
C              ExSr      AddDurSubr
C              EndIf

C              Return    SubrDate

 ************Subroutine AddDurSubr************
C    AddDurSubr    BegSr

C              Select

C              When      SubrDurCode = '*YEARS'
C                        Or SubrDurCode = '*Y'
C              AddDur    SubrDurAmt:*Y SubrDate
```

continued

FIGURE 3.19 *CONTINUED*

```
C                       When         SubrDurCode = '*MONTHS'
C                       Or SubrDurCode = '*M'
C                       AddDur       SubrDurAmt:*M SubrDate

C                       When         SubrDurCode = '*DAYS'
C                       Or SubrDurCode = '*D'
C                       AddDur       SubrDurAmt:*D SubrDate

C                       EndSl

C                       EndSr

P AddDate          E
```

```
    .
    .
    .
```

I won't fully explain the inner workings of this procedure here; I'll just explore how to use AddDate from an invoking program. The following code adds 10 days to an order date to obtain an estimated shipping date:

```
C                       Eval         EstShpDate = AddDate( OrdDate:
C                                                  10:
C                                                  '*D' )
```

The '*D' is a duration code. The procedure accepts the same set of duration codes that are permitted in the AddDur and SubDur instructions in ILE RPG. For example, because ILE RPG permits a duration code of *DAYS, I could have accomplished the same thing with the following code:

```
C                       Eval         EstShpDate = AddDate( OrdDate:
C                                                  10:
C                                                  '*DAYS' )
```

Also, because ILE RPG permits mixed case with these duration codes, I could have spelled *DAYS as *Days or *dAyS.

The AddDate procedure also lets me add up to three durations. For example, I can use the following code to test whether a user is eligible to be vested in the company's pension plan:

```
C                       If           AddDate( HireDate:
C                                           10: '*Years':
C                                            1: '*Days'  )
C                                    > TodaysDate
C                       ExSr         ProcVestedEmp
C                       EndIf
```

In the first example, I pass three parameters to procedure AddDate, and in the second example I pass five parameters. This is made possible by the Options(*NoPass) keyword.

In the prototype at **A** in Figure 3.19, the fourth through seventh parameters specify Options(*NoPass). The rule is: once you specify Options(*NoPass) for a particular parameter, you must specify it for all subsequent parameters. This is because suppressing an Options(*NoPass) parameter requires the user to suppress all subsequent parameters as well.

You'll recall that with Options(*Omit), we tested for an omitted parameter by checking whether the address of the parameter was equal to *Null. With Options(*NoPass), we simply use the %Parms built-in function to count the number of parameters passed. (Note: This technique won't work for Options(*Omit) because an omitted parameter is still counted as being passed via the %Parms built-in function. Similarly, the technique of testing the address of a passed parameter for *Null, which we used with Options(*Omit), won't work with Options(*NoPass).) At **B**, the number of parameters passed is saved in a field called Parms. The number of parameters passed is tested at **C** and **D**.

Summary

ILE RPG subprocedures are extremely useful because they support parameter passing and have local variables. And because subprocedures are named in D-specs, their names aren't limited in size. So you can give them meaningful names.

Subprocedures let you pass parameters by value and read-only reference as well as by reference. When you pass parameters by value and read-only reference, you can use expressions for them.

You can also use the ExtPgm keyword to prototype OPM programs. By specifying the Const keyword for those parameters that the OPM program does not change, you can take advantage of the fact that parameters passed by read-only reference can be expressions.

Keywords Options(*Omit) and Options(*NoPass) provide a rich set of options for parameter suppression.

Chapter 4

Service Programs

Service programs are the ILE repositories of general routines. As a general rule, you create service programs to contain procedures that are needed by more than one ILE program.

As an alternative to using service programs, you might bind a module by copy into all the programs that need it. But this approach presents some difficulties. For example, if I make a change to a module that's bound by copy, I have to rebind — that is, reissue the CrtPgm command for — all the programs that use that module. This means I must keep track of which programs use which modules. Also, binding a module by copy into multiple programs is inefficient memory utilization if more than one program may use the module concurrently.

With service programs, only one copy of any particular module is in memory at a time. More important, you can change a service program without having to rebind — as long as you don't change the number or types of parameters that are passed to the various procedures in the service program. Changing a service program without rebinding to the programs and service programs that use it can be tricky. Later in this chapter, I'll explain why.

Creating and Using Service Programs

A service program is a different object type than a program. Its type is *SrvPgm, and it's created via the CrtSrvPgm (Create Service Program) command. Recall how Figure 1.2 in Chapter 1 showed the process of creating an ILE program. The analogous picture for service programs (Figure 4.1) is quite similar. Actually, the only difference is the final step, in which we issue a CrtSrvPgm command instead of a CrtPgm command.

FIGURE 4.1

Creating an RPG IV Service Program

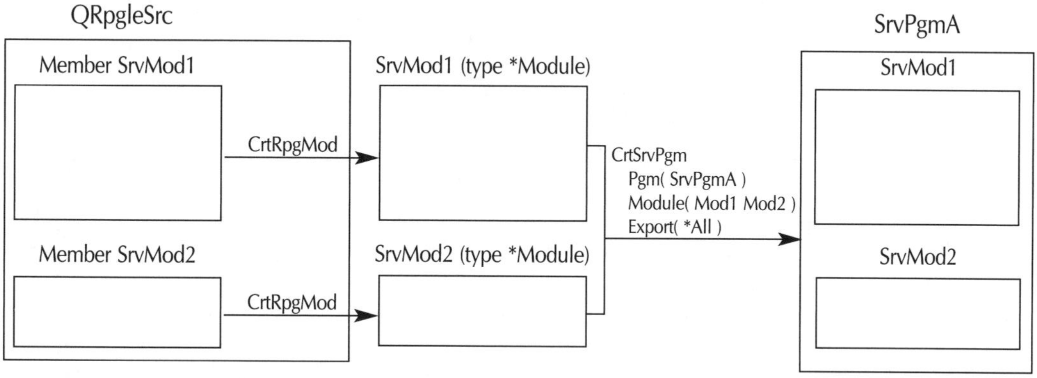

Once you create a service program, you can use it in an ILE RPG program, as Figure 4.2 shows. You start by creating a module object (in this case, PgmMod1) via the CrtRpgMod command (PDM option 15). Next, you use the CrtPgm command to incorporate the service program into the program object. You use the CrtPgm command's BndSrvPgm parameter to tell the binder which service program (or programs) to use.

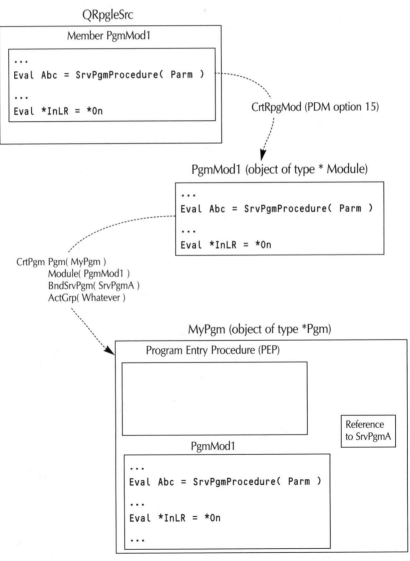

FIGURE 4.2

Using a Service Program in an ILE Program

Notice that a reference to the service program is placed into program MyPgm. This is why IBM refers to this process as *bind by reference*. Later in this chapter, we'll explore the nature of this reference more thoroughly. For now, simply understand that (unlike with bind by copy) the service program isn't copied into the program object. Rather, a reference is made to the service program. This is why you can change the service program without having to rebind the program.

Service programs can be invoked only from an ILE program or from another service program. In particular, you can't invoke any service program procedures with the AS/400 Call command. Therefore, you can't directly invoke a service program procedure or gain access to service program data from an AS/400 command line.

Can OPM Programs Use Service Programs?

The short answer to this question is *no*. However, OPM programs can call ILE programs, which can invoke procedures in a service program. Therefore, if you want an OPM program to have access to a service program, you must write an ILE "wrapper" program that invokes the service program on behalf of the OPM program.

Service Program Exports

A service program makes its procedures and data available to procedures running outside it as *exports*. In Figure 4.2, procedure SrvPgmProcedure must be an export to be invoked from ILE program MyPgm.

To better explain the concept of exports, I'll use the terms *candidate procedures* and *candidate data*. (Note that these terms aren't official ILE terminology.) Candidate procedures are of two types. First, ILE RPG main procedures (if any) are candidate procedures. Recall that the name of an ILE RPG main procedure is the same as its module name. (It's unusual to have main procedures in service programs; however, they're not precluded.) The other candidate procedures are ILE RPG subprocedures that use the Export keyword in their procedure begin statement. Candidate data are any data specifications that use the Export keyword.

Candidate procedures and data are always available throughout a service program. Also, when you create a service program specifying Export(*All), all the candidate procedures and data are available (or exported) to other ILE programs and service programs that use this service program. Before we explore how to limit the procedure and data exports to some proper subset of the candidates, let's discuss why we'd want to limit these exports in the first place.

Why Limit Your Exports?

Imagine you've been asked to design and develop a service program that implements a business calendar for your company. A business calendar is a calendar that records so-called "business" and "non-business" days. For example, if your company considers weekends and holidays to be non-business days, they're recorded as such in the business calendar.

In your analysis, you define two categories of functions that must be available in the business calendar service program: maintenance and calculations. The maintenance functions let you flexibly define non-business days. Here are some sample functions that fall into this category:

- AddBusHoliday(Date) defines Date as a non-business day.
- RmvBusHoliday(Date) reverses the AddBusHoliday definition for Date.
- AddRepeatingNonBusinessDay(DayOfWeek) specifies that Saturday (for example) is a repeating non-business day.
- RmvRepeatingNonBusinessDay(DayOfWeek) reverses the AddRepeatingNonBusinessDay definition for a particular DayOfWeek.

Here are some sample functions that fall into the calculation category:

- AddBusDays(Date: NoOfDays) adds NoOfDays business days to Date.
- SubBusDays(Date: NoOfDays) subtracts NoOfDays business days from Date.
- ElapsedBusDays(Date1: Date2) computes the number of elapsed business days between two dates.

Now consider two basic design possibilities. First, you can implement an exception-based database, which contains one record for each non-business day. Second, you can implement a full 365/366 records per year database, which has one record for each day of the year, regardless of whether the day is a business or non-business day. Given the preceding set of functions, you decide to implement the business calendar database with exception records. In other words, you decide that records in your database represent non-business days.

However, although the current set of functions works fine with an exception-based database, you worry that future requirements might make a full 365/366 records per year database necessary. You could implement the full database now in case you need it in the future. But another approach to this problem represents a compromise between the two solutions.

The idea is to use design layering with an exception-type database (Figure 4.3). The functions that you identify to be available in the business calendar service program appear inside the box labeled "Exported layer." These functions use other functions that appear inside a box labeled "Private layer." The functions inside the private layer work directly with the database. This design allows for a specialized interface (or set of parameters) that needs to be passed between procedures in the exported layer and the private layer.

The procedures defined in the exported layer are available to ILE programs and other service programs. Procedures defined in the private layer are available only within the service program. However, because the procedures in the private layer are needed by multiple procedures in the exported layer, you must make the procedures in the private layer available throughout the service program.

FIGURE 4.3

Design Layering with an Exception-type Database

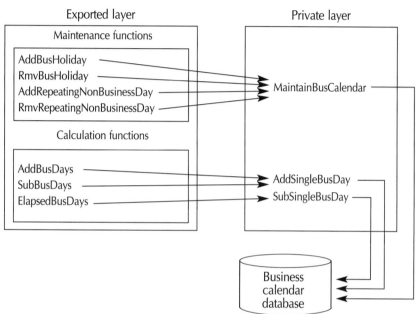

Thus, you would specify the Export keyword in these procedures, but you wouldn't want to make the procedures globally available outside the service program. If you made procedures inside the private layer available globally, your ability to make changes (such as changing from an exception to a 365/366 days per year database) would be seriously hampered. For example, you couldn't freely add new parameters passed from the exported-layer procedures to the private-layer procedures without also making sure that all programs and service programs that use these private-layer procedures pass the newly added parameters.

Assuming you keep the private-layer procedures private, the process of changing from an exception-based to a full 365/366 days per year database is greatly simplified: you just rewrite the procedures in the private layer and change the procedures in the exported layer to implement any new interfaces between the layers. You don't need to worry about changing anything outside the service program itself.

How to Limit Your Exports

Let's review what I mean by candidate exports. A candidate export consists of the following:

- ILE RPG main procedures (if any)
- procedures that use the Export keyword in their procedure begin statements
- data specifications (ILE RPG D-specs) that specify the Export keyword

Recall also that candidates are available throughout a service program, and specifying Export(*All) when creating a service program makes all the candidates available to ILE programs and service programs that use the service program.

To limit exports to a subset of the candidate exports, you must place *binder language commands* into a source physical file member. You can obtain SEU prompting and syntax checking for binder language if you specify a source type of Bnd. Also, the default name for the source physical file containing binder language members is QSrvSrc. I've found it most convenient to place my binder language source into a source physical file with this name and then give the members the same name that I use for the service program.

Figure 4.4 shows the binder language source that limits the exports in a service program to Proc1, Proc2, Data1, and Proc3. Any candidate procedure or data name specified in the list of exports is available outside the service program. Any candidate that's not specified in the list of exports isn't available outside the service program.

FIGURE 4.4

Binder Language Limiting Exports to
Proc1, Proc2, Data1, and Proc3

```
StrPgmExp        PgmLvl( *Current )

Export           'Proc1'
Export           'Proc2'
Export           'Data1'
Export           'Proc3'
EndPgmExp
```

Assuming the source physical file member containing the binder language source of Figure 4.4 is QSrvSrc and QSrvSrc is currently in your library list, the command to create this service program would look like this:

```
CrtSrvPgm  SrvPgm( MySrvPgm )
           Module( list-of-modules )
           Export( *SrcFile )
           SrcFile( QSrvSrc )
```

Note that binder language source isn't compiled. It's only referenced in the CrtSrvPgm command, as shown here.

The Export Table and Signatures

Let's continue with the example of exporting Proc1, Proc2, Data1, and Proc3. After the CrtSrvPgm command is executed, the service program is created. One of its components is the *export table*, which contains the list of exports for the service program. IBM doesn't give us the exact format of this table, but Figure 4.5 shows roughly what type of information goes into it.

FIGURE 4.5

The Export Table

Export name	Export location
Proc1	Offset X'5C2E'
Proc2	Offset X'6DF7'
Data1	Offset X'647A'
Proc3	Offset X'4F2F'

First, note that the export table is ordered; Proc1 is first, Proc2 is second, and so on. The order of entries in the export table is significant for *signature generation,* as you'll see in a moment. The column labeled "Export location" simply shows my guesses as to other information that goes in this table. It's not important to know the details of this other information, but note that there's enough information for the system to determine what it needs to know about an export (such as its starting location).

Given a set of exports and an order for those exports, the system generates a unique *signature.* This signature is analogous to the familiar file levels. The system generates a unique level for each file based on a given record format name, a list of field names (in a particular order), and types and lengths associated with those fields. Any change to any aspect of these four things (record format names, names of fields, order of fields, type and length of fields) results in a different level. Similarly, any change in the names, order, or number of exports results in a different signature for a service program.

To carry this analogy further, let's expand on how the system works with levels in files. When you compile a program, the system saves the levels associated with the files used by that program in the program object itself. When the program opens the file, the system compares the level in the program object with the level in the file. If they're not equal, the system sends escape message "CPF4131 Level Check on *file-name* in library *lib-name* with member *member-name*." Similarly, if an ILE program uses a procedure in a service program, the system stores the signature of the service program in the program object. When the ILE program is activated, the system checks to see whether the signature stored in the program appears in a list of signatures stored in the service program. If the signature isn't in the list, the system sends escape message "MCH4431 Signature violation."

In the case of files, it's not important to understand the exact algorithm for generating the level. You need to know only what factors go into calculating the level. For files, it's the record format names, the field names, the order of the fields in the format, and the types and lengths of the fields. Change any of these factors, and you change the file level. Similarly, the factors that create service program signatures are the number of exports, their names, and their order in the export table. Change the names of any of the exports, the number of exports, or their order, and you change the signature.

Binder language source lets us specify both the names and the order of the exports. The order of the exports is the order in which they appear in the binder language source. When we specify Export(*All), we relinquish this control over the order of our exports. We have no knowledge of this order in this case.

Returning now to our example, suppose it's six months after you've created your service program with its four exports and you need to add two new exports: Proc4 and Proc5. Your first inclination might be to re-create the service program with binder source, as in Figure 4.6.

FIGURE 4.6

Adding Exports Proc4 and Proc5 (First Inclination)

```
StrPgmExp              PgmLvl( *Current )

Export                 'Proc1'
Export                 'Proc2'
Export                 'Data1'
Export                 'Proc3'
Export                 'Proc4'
Export                 'Proc5'
EndPgmExp
```

But this generates a new signature. Any programs or service programs that use this service program will now fail due to a signature check.

Service programs let us generate binder source that addresses this problem. Figure 4.7 shows the proper way to code your binder source.

FIGURE 4.7

Adding Exports Proc4 and Proc5 (Correct Solution)

```
Ⓐ  StrPgmExp           PgmLvl( *Current )

    Export             'Proc1'
    Export             'Proc2'
    Export             'Data1'
    Export             'Proc3'
    Export             'Proc4'
    Export             'Proc5'
    EndPgmExp


Ⓑ  StrPgmExp           PgmLvl( *Prv )

    Export             'Proc1'
    Export             'Proc2'
    Export             'Data1'
    Export             'Proc3'
    EndPgmExp
```

The binder language source in Figure 4.7 actually results in the generation of two signatures. At **A,** the StrPgmExp statement specifies PgmLvl(*Current). There can be only one *Current set of exports. It should specify all the exports for the service program and define the contents and order of the export table.

Notice, at **B**, I specify PgmLvl(*Prv). There can be any number of *Prv (previous) sets of exports. Notice also that the *Prv set of exports consists of the original four exports in their original order. Moreover, the *Current set features the original four exports along with the newest exports (Proc4 and Proc5) added at the end. The binder language source in this figure generates two signatures. The *Current signature will be different from the original signature. But the *Prv signature will be identical to the original signature because it's the same set of export names in the same order as the original. Because the original signature is stored in the service program, there's no need to rebind programs and service programs that use this service program.

Using this scheme, you can add new exports any number of times. After a while, you'll have programs and service programs that have recorded not only the new signature but all the previous signatures as well. If you then needed to add two more exports (Proc6 and Data2), you'd re-create the service program with the binder language source in Figure 4.8, which generates a new signature corresponding to the *Current set of exports plus the two original signatures of Figure 4.7.

FIGURE 4.8
Adding Exports Proc6 and Data2

```
StrPgmExp        PgmLvl( *Current )
Export           'Proc1'
Export           'Proc2'
Export           'Data1'
Export           'Proc3'
Export           'Proc4'
Export           'Proc5'
Export           'Proc6'
Export           'Data2'
EndPgmExp

StrPgmExp        PgmLvl( *Prv )
Export           'Proc1'
Export           'Proc2'
Export           'Data1'
Export           'Proc3'
Export           'Proc4'
Export           'Proc5'
EndPgmExp

StrPgmExp        PgmLvl( *Prv )
Export           'Proc1'
Export           'Proc2'
Export           'Data1'
Export           'Proc3'
EndPgmExp
```

The process for adding new exports is completely mechanical:

- Use SEU copy to copy the *Current set of exports.
- Add the new exports to the end of the first set of *Current exports.
- Change the second set of *Current exports to specify PgmLvl(*Prv).

It's important to execute the process exactly this way. The *Current set of exports should always begin with the previous set of exports followed by the new exports. The reason for this involves how the system stores the reference to the export in the programs and service programs that invoke procedures and use exported data in the service program.

Recall, the *Current exports determine the names and order of exports in the export table. Now suppose you code the following ILE RPG instruction.

```
C                       Eval      Fld = Proc2( X )
```

The binder doesn't store the name Proc2 in the program object. Instead, it stores the export table number for this procedure (in this case, 2). When the ILE RPG program is activated, the system knows that it must execute the second entry in the export table when the above Eval statement is executed. Now it should be clear why the original exports must be in the same order when you re-create a service program. Otherwise, the second entry might not correspond to Proc2, and you'd have a real mess on your hands.

Is Bind by Reference Slower Than Bind by Copy?

Tests show no significant speed difference between invoking a procedure in a service program and invoking a procedure in a module bound by copy. However, when you use a service program, there's a slight performance hit when you activate it because the system must load, allocate, and initialize storage for all the modules in the service program. There can even be a cascading effect because if the service program invokes procedures or uses exported data from other service programs, they will have to be loaded as well. Having said all this, I've experienced no significant performance problems at program activation time. This is particularly true because of today's larger, faster AS/400 systems.

When to Use Export(*All)

When you specify Export(*All) in the CrtSrvPgm command, you're telling the system that you aren't using binder language source. Instead, you want to export all the candidates. This approach is certainly easier initially because you don't have to generate any binder language source. However, specifying Export(*All) relinquishes your control of signatures. So you have no way to add new exports in the future without rebinding all the programs and service programs that use your service program.

While testing your service program, you should use Export(*All). Specifying Export(*All) is easiest if you never expect to add new exports to your service program. However, saying you don't expect to add new exports to your service program is like a user reassuring you that there will never be more than 100 line items in a given invoice. Such statements should be taken with a grain of salt. I strongly suggest that you use binder source with all your service programs.

Should I Export Data from a Service Program?

Exporting data means that all programs that use a service program within a job have access to that data. This is usually a bad policy because it's too hard to control the content of data across programs. For this reason, I recommend you avoid this practice in most instances. The sole exception to this rule (in my experience), where a service program containing exported data can be used to your advantage, involves a kind of "blackboard" communication vehicle between a program that causes a database trigger to be invoked and the trigger program itself. Appendix C describes a service program that uses this technique.

Summary

Service programs are the ILE repositories of general-purpose routines. When a program or service program uses procedures or data from a service program, the system stores a reference to the service program in the invoking program or service program. This process is called *bind by reference*.

The system generates a *signature* for a service program based on the number, names, and order of the *exports* (i.e., procedures and data available outside the service program) and stores that signature in the invoking program and service program. The signature is analogous to file levels. If you follow the steps outlined in this chapter when using binder source, you can safely add new exports to a service program without having to rebind the programs and service programs that use it.

Chapter 5

Activation Groups

Before launching into the details of activation groups, let's consider an example of when you might use them. In the order entry screen in Figure 5.1, function key F8 takes you to the accounts payable application.

FIGURE 5.1

An Order Entry Screen

```
 7/14/00                      Order Entry                    MCRAVITZ
 12:34:27                                                    S100B54R


    Order No.      123456    For Cust#    54321 Perry's Pantaloons


        Item
          No     Description                    Qty

    -   SK1234   Long, sleek blue pantaloon      30
    -   SK4321   Short, stubby pink pantaloon    15
    -   SK5318   Weird but stylish grey shorts   28
    -   SK2742   Garish green taffeta jumper     30
                                                            MORE...
    Use the following line to add an item to the order
    _____

    F8=Accounts Payable for This Customer   F10=Complete Order
    F3=Exit   F12=Cancel Order
```

Typically, order entry and accounts payable applications are designed and developed separately. They may even be purchased from separate third parties. This can result in some difficulties when two independently developed applications each have their own set of overrides and commitment-control definitions in effect.

For example, suppose a shared open data path override is in effect for the Customer file while the user is in the order entry screen. If the application jumps to (i.e., calls a program in) the accounts payable application, that shared override will remain in effect. An RPG program in the accounts payable application might assume that the Customer file is initially positioned at the first customer record in the file, but this might not be the case if a shared open data path override is in effect.

To be safe, the order entry application should, before invoking the accounts payable application, temporarily delete any overrides to files used by both applications. It should reissue the overrides when the user returns from the called application.

A similar problem occurs if both applications use commitment control because they'll both be within the scope of the same commitment definition. You almost never want this when two applications are designed and developed independently. If you have uncommitted transactions, you probably need them to remain uncommitted; otherwise, you'd have committed them by now. Unfortunately, the only safe way to avoid the problem of both applications being within the same commitment definition is to commit uncommitted transactions and then end commitment control temporarily until control is returned from the accounts payable system. This method is clearly untenable.

Before the advent of ILE, you could use group jobs to solve this problem — if you were running interactively. But group jobs use a tremendous amount of resources, and setting them up is quite complex. IBM invented activation groups to solve these problems in an ILE environment.

Activation Groups Defined

Activation groups are environments within a job. The phrase "within a job" is important here. In other words, if JobA has an activation group called A and JobB has an activation group called A, they're two different activation groups even though they have the same name.

There are three distinct types of activation groups:

- default
- named
- *New

Every job has a default activation group. In fact, each job has two default activation groups. One of them is used by IBM system programs behind the scenes and has very little direct bearing on our everyday lives as ILE developers. Hence, we ordinarily refer to the *default activation group* as if there were only one. Whenever I refer to the default activation group, I mean the one in which user programs run (not the one in which IBM system programs run) unless I specifically state otherwise.

Of the three types of activation groups, the default activation group behaves most like OPM environments before ILE. The default activation group is created when a job is activated, and it remains active until the job is terminated. The programmer has no direct control over creation or deletion of the default activation group.

A program or service program runs in the default activation group whenever one of the following is true:

- The program is an OPM program.
- The program was created with DftActGrp(*Yes) specified on the CrtBnd*Xxx* command.
- The program or service program is invoked from a program or service program running in the default activation group and was created with ActGrp(*Caller) specified on the CrtBnd*Xxx*, CrtPgm, or CrtSrvPgm command. (Note, this includes programs created with ActGrp(*Caller) invoked from an AS/400 command line because the command line monitor itself runs in the default activation group.)

A program or service program runs in a *named activation group* if one of the following statements is true:

- The program or service program was created with ActGrp(*name*) specified in the CrtBnd*Xxx*, CrtPgm, or CrtSrvPgm command, where *name* is the name of the activation group.
- The program or service program is invoked by a program or service program running in a named activation group and was created with ActGrp(*Caller) specified in the CrtBnd*Xxx*, CrtPgm, or CrtSrvPgm command.

A program runs in a *New activation group if one of the following two statements is true:

- The program or service program was created with ActGrp(*New) specified in the CrtBnd*Xxx*, CrtPgm, or CrtSrvPgm command.
- The program or service program is invoked by a program or service program running in a *New activation group and was created with ActGrp(*Caller) specified in the CrtBnd*Xxx*, CrtPgm, or CrtSrvPgm command.

Calling a Program Running in *New

A program created to run in a *New activation group exhibits special behavior. If I call a program that runs in a *New activation group, the system creates an activation group with a 10-character system-generated name and then activates my program. Notice, I didn't say anything about the activation group in which the calling program runs because it doesn't matter. Even if the calling program is running in a *New activation group, the system will still create *another* *New activation group to run the program.

Let's suppose further that this program is an ILE RPG program. When the program ends, the system deletes the activation group whether the program ends with its LR indicator set on or off. This is a potential performance trap. Ordinarily, you'd code an RPG program to return with LR set off to improve performance. But if you repeatedly call such a program and it runs in a *New activation group, you'll experience extremely sluggish performance. Not only does the system deactivate the program after the program returns control to the calling program, but it deletes the *New activation group. Each subsequent call results in the system re-creating the *New activation group and reactivating the program.

To make matters worse, the CrtPgm command uses ActGrp(*New) as its default value. So if you use this command, you must explicitly code the ActGrp parameter to avoid this pitfall.

One way to avoid this performance trap is to change the default for the ActGrp parameter on the CrtPgm command. It's best to avoid changing an actual IBM-supplied command. You can, however, create a copy of the CrtPgm command with the CrtDupObj (Create Duplicate Object) command and place the copied command in a user library that appears in the system library list ahead of IBM library QSYS. (Note, you can change the default system library list by specifying SysVal(QSysLibl) on the ChgSysVal, or Change System Value, command.) After you've created a duplicate of the CrtPgm command, you should change the command default of this newly created command. Here's a sample command that changes the duplicated CrtPgm command default to specify ActGrp(*Caller):

```
ChgCmdDft  Cmd( OurLib/CrtPgm )
           NewDft( 'ActGrp(*Caller)' )
```

Override Parameters and Activation Groups

The AS/400 supports override commands for each supported file type. These are the file override commands available on the AS/400:

- OvrDbf (Override with Database File)
- OvrDktf (Override with Diskette File)
- OvrDspf (Override with Display File)
- OvrIcff (Override with ICF File)
- OvrPrtf (Override with Printer File)
- OvrSavf (Override with Save File)
- OvrTapf (Override with Tape File)

(Two other override commands are available, but they don't pertain to AS/400 *File types or to this discussion.)

You use these commands to temporarily change various defaults. For example, the OvrDbf command can instruct an RPG program that's expecting to use a file called Orders to instead use another file whose name is OrdersSw.

For the purposes of this discussion, I classify the parameters in these override commands into four categories: the File parameter, the override parameters, the Share parameter, and the scoping parameters.

The File parameter simply tells the system what file is being overridden. If you're overriding a file referenced in an ILE RPG program, the File parameter will match the file name of the F-spec for the file in question.

I define the override parameter category as a catch-all. In other words, all parameters in the override commands that don't fall within the other three parameter categories are override parameters.

The Share Parameter

The override commands' Share parameter tells whether you want open data path sharing to be in effect for the override. When you issue a shared override, it means you want programs to share the open data path for the file in question. An *open data path* is the data structure that the system uses to keep track of open files within a job. As soon as a program opens a file, the system creates an open data path in memory to hold information about that open file. One key piece of information saved in the open data path is the current position within the file.

When the file is first opened, the open data path is set to point to the first record in the file. If open data path sharing is in effect, the first program opening the file performs a full file open, which includes allocating memory for the open data path as well as filling in information to the open data path. If this first program then calls a second program that also opens the file, the open will be far faster because the open data path is being shared.

In this scenario, however, programs must be more careful about file positioning. In Figure 5.2, CL program ClPgmA issues a shared override for the Customer file — by executing the command OvrDbf Customer Share(*Yes) — and then calls RPG program RpgPgmA.

FIGURE 5.2

An Illustration of Shared Override

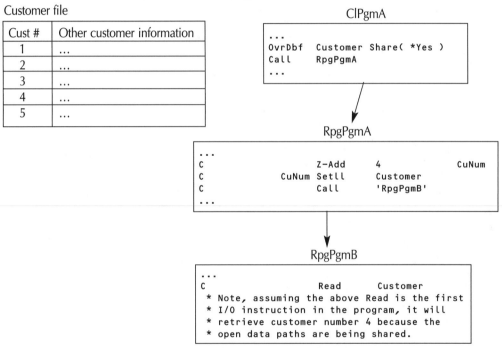

RpgPgmA issues a Setll (Set lower limit) instruction for customer number 4 and then calls RpgPgmB. Notice that the comment in RpgPgmB states that the program is positioned at customer number 4, not customer number 1, when it opens the file. So the Read will retrieve customer 4, assuming this read is the first I/O performed to the Customer file in the program.

In general, with open data path sharing, a called program must not assume initial positioning. Moreover, the calling program must not assume that it's positioned at the same record that it was before the call.

The OvrScope Parameter

The fourth category of override command parameters is the scoping parameters: OvrScope (Override scope) and OpnScope (Open scope). The OvrScope parameter controls which programs in the call stack will be aware of the override. OvrScope has three possible values:

- *ActGrpDfn (Activation group definition)
- *CallLvl (Caller level)
- *Job

Specifying OvrScope(*ActGrpDfn), which is the default for OvrScope, means:

- If the override is issued from the default activation group, it's a *CallLvl override.
- If the override is issued from a named or *New activation group, the OvrScope(*ActGrpDfn) override is scoped to that activation group.

Because specifying OvrScope(*ActGrpDfn) from the default activation group implies the override will be a *CallLvl override, I'll address this behavior in a moment when I discuss OvrScope(*CallLvl). For now, let's confine our attention to the case in which the override specifying OvrScope(*ActGrpDfn) is issued from a named or *New activation group.

If an override issued in a named or *New activation group specifies OvrScope(*ActGrpDfn), it is seen within the activation group only. Figure 5.3 shows what happens when an override specifying OvrScope(*ActGrpDfn) is issued in a named or *New activation group. In scenario 1, an override issued from program Pgm1 is running in a named or *New activation group. Program Pgm2 doesn't see the override because Pgm2 is running in a different activation group from that of Pgm1 and because the override was scoped to the activation group only. Program Pgm3 does see the override because it runs in the same activation group as Pgm1.

In scenario 2, both Pgm1 and Pgm3 see the override after Pgm2 issues it because they're both running in the same activation group as Pgm2. This is true even though Pgm2 is completely out of the call stack at the time Pgm1 and Pgm3 become aware of the override.

An override issued from a named or *New activation group and specifying OvrScope(*ActGrpDfn) remains in effect until either the activation group is deleted, the job ends, or a DltOvr (Delete Override) command is issued to delete the override.

Now let's talk about OvrScope(*CallLvl). Before the introduction of ILE in OS/400 V2R3, all overrides were caller-level (*CallLvl) overrides. In fact, it wasn't until V2R3 that the OvrScope and OpnScope parameters became available. A *CallLvl override is seen from the point of issue forward in the call stack. Figure 5.4 illustrates this point.

FIGURE 5.3

Override Scoped to the Activation Group

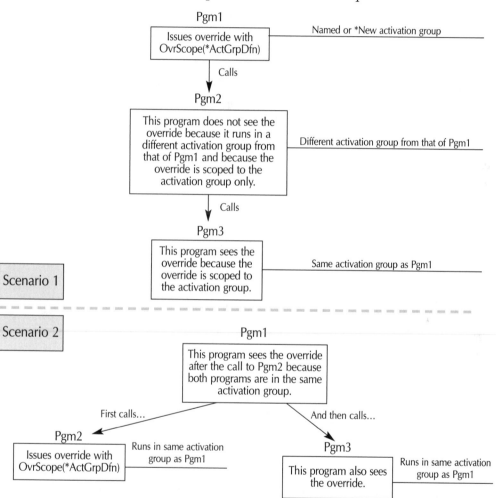

FIGURE 5.4

*CallLvl Overrides

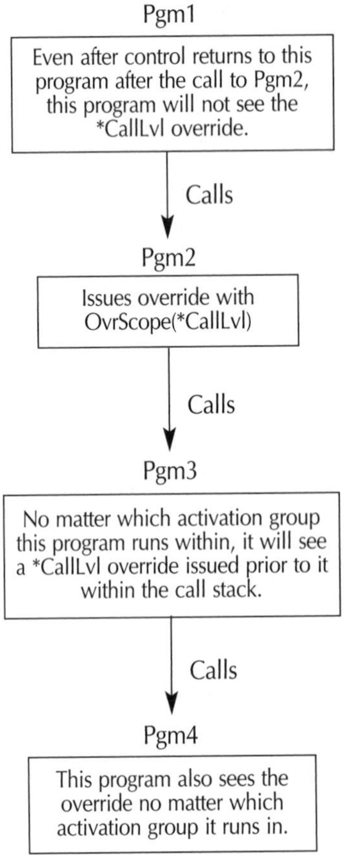

Pgm1

> Even after control returns to this
> program after the call to Pgm2,
> this program will not see the
> *CallLvl override.

Calls ↓

Pgm2

> Issues override with
> OvrScope(*CallLvl)

Calls ↓

Pgm3

> No matter which activation group
> this program runs within, it will see
> a *CallLvl override issued prior to it
> within the call stack.

Calls ↓

Pgm4

> This program also sees the
> override no matter which
> activation group it runs in.

Notice, I coded the second program (Pgm2) to issue the *CallLvl override to show that when you specify OvrScope(*CallLvl), the override won't be seen before the point of issue in the call stack. (Contrast this with scenario 2 of Figure 5.3.) Pgm1 won't see the override even after control returns to it after the call to Pgm2. *CallLvl overrides are automatically deleted when the call stack entry that issues the override returns control to the previous call stack entry.

Notice that I didn't bother to tell you what activation groups any of the programs in this example were running within. For the purposes of the current discussion, activation group considerations don't matter. A *CallLvl override is seen from the point of issue forward in the call stack regardless of the mix of activation groups involved.

The third and last OvrScope parameter value to discuss is *Job. This one is simple. A call stack entry issuing an override specifying OvrScope(*Job) is seen by all other call stack entries regardless of their relative position in the call stack or the activation groups in which they run. An override specifying OvrScope(*Job) is in effect until the job is completed or until a DltOvr command is issued to delete the override.

The OpnScope Parameter

The other scoping parameter is the OpnScope parameter, which is operational when a Share(*Yes) override is seen by the program. (Otherwise, it is ignored.) OpnScope determines which of two levels of sharing takes place. The first level is job-level sharing, which is in effect when OpnScope(*Job) has been specified. OpnScope(*Job) means all call stack entries that see the override will share the same open data path. Alternatively, when a Share(*Yes) override specifies OpnScope(*ActGrpDfn), all call stack entries that see the override will share the open data path with all other call stack entries that run in the same activation group. Figure 5.5 shows how this works.

FIGURE 5.5

*How OpnScope(*ActGrpDfn) Works*

Pgm1

| Issues a Share(*Yes) override to file X with OvrScope(*CallLvl) and OpnScope(*ActGrpDfn). It then reads the first record in file X. | Runs in activation group A |

Calls

Pgm2

| Reads file X sequentially. It reads the first record because it shares only within its own activation group. | Runs in activation group B |

Calls

Pgm3

| Sequentially reads file X. It reads the second record because it is sharing the open data path with Pgm2. | Runs in activation group B |

Calls

Pgm4

| Sequentially reads file X. It reads the second record because it is sharing the open data path with Pgm1. | Runs in activation group A |

Pgm1 issues a Share(*Yes) override to a file called X. Pgm1 is running in named activation group A, and the override specifies OvrScope(*CallLvl) and OpnScope(*ActGrpDfn). Pgm1 then reads the first record in file X and calls Pgm2, which is running in named activation group B. Pgm2 sees the override because the OvrScope value is *CallLvl. Nevertheless, Pgm2 sequentially reads the *first* record from file X, not the second record, as you might expect. The reason for this is Pgm2 is sharing only within its own activation group (B) because the OpnScope parameter specifies *ActGrpDfn.

Now Pgm2 calls Pgm3, which is running in named activation group B. Pgm3 shares the open data path with Pgm2 because they're both running in the same activation group. Because Pgm2 has already read the first record in file X, the next sequential read issued against that same open data path will retrieve the second record. That's why Pgm3 reads the second record in file X.

Finally, Pgm3 calls Pgm4. Again, Pgm4 sees the override because OvrScope(*CallLvl) has been specified. Because Pgm4 is running in activation group A and OpnScope has been specified as *ActGrpDfn, Pgm4 shares the open data path with Pgm1. Because Pgm1 has read the first record in file X, Pgm4 will read the second record.

Now, suppose Pgm1 used an OpnScope value of *Job instead of *ActGrpDfn. In this case, the open data path would be shared across activation groups. Pgm2 would read record 2, Pgm3 would read record 3, and Pgm4 would read record 4.

Finally, suppose Pgm1 had specified OvrScope(*ActGrpDfn) and kept OpnScope(*ActGrpDfn). In that case, Pgm2 and Pgm3 wouldn't see the override. No open data path sharing would take place for these two programs, and they would therefore read record 1. Pgm4 would see the override because it's running in the same activation group as Pgm1. And because it's sharing the open data path with Pgm1, Pgm4 would read record 2.

Now look at Figure 5.6. A Share(*Yes) override specifying an OvrScope and an OpnScope value of *ActGrpDfn is being issued from the default activation group. Remember, because the override is issued from the default activation group, the override scope is actually *CallLvl, and a *CallLvl override is always seen from the point of issue within the call stack forward. Therefore, Pgm2 and Pgm3 see the override.

Because Pgm2 and Pgm3 are running in the same named activation group (activation group A), they'll share the open data path. Because the OpnScope value is *ActGrpDfn, Pgm2 and Pgm3 will use their own open data path, which is confined to activation group A. This is why Pgm2 reads record 1 instead of record 2 (because it's not sharing the open data path with Pgm1). In Figure 5.6, if Pgm1 had specified OpnScope(*Job), Pgm2 and Pgm3 would share the open data path with Pgm1. Pgm2 would read record 2, and Pgm3 would read record 3.

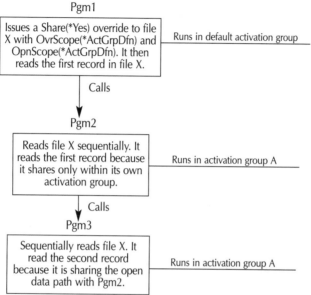

FIGURE 5.6
Share(*Yes) from the Default Activation Group

Let's summarize the principles for scenarios with mixed activation groups and Share(*Yes) overrides:

- The OvrScope parameter determines whether a call stack entry sees the override.
- The OpnScope parameter applies only to Share(*Yes) overrides and determines which of two degrees of sharing takes place in the event that the call stack entry sees the override. The two degrees of sharing are job level, which occurs when OpnScope(*Job) is specified, and sharing within the activation group, which occurs when OpnScope(*ActGrpDfn) is specified.

Activation Groups and Commitment Control

The rules for commitment control scoping are simpler than those for override scoping. You start commitment control by executing the StrCmtCtl (Start Commitment Control) command. The commitment definition scope is controlled by the CmtScope parameter on this command. The CmtScope parameter accepts one of two possible values: *ActGrp or *Job.

If you use StrCmtCtl specifying CmtScope(*ActGrp), which is the default, the commitment definition applies to the entire activation group in which it was issued — but only to this activation group. This is true even when StrCmtCtl is issued in the default activation group. The commitment control definition remains in effect within that activation group until the EndCmtCtl (End Commitment Control) command is issued. EndCmtCtl can be issued from any program running in the activation group in which the StrCmtCtl command was issued.

Specifying *Job for the CmtScope parameter means the commitment definition extends to the entire job. This type of commitment definition crosses all activation group boundaries. It is ended when the job ends or when any program in the job issues the EndCmtCtl command.

Reclaiming Activation Groups

Before ILE, the RclRsc (Reclaim Resources) command functioned as a basic clean-up method. You typically used it with RPG programs that ended with the LR indicator set off. (This leaves the program activated; the files remain open, and the variables remain unmodified.) A subsequent call to such a program doesn't require any files to be opened because they're already opened. Also, a program that ends with LR set off must be serially reusable. This means it can't depend on the RPG cycle to reinitialize any variables because its variables are unmodified from the previous call. Therefore, such a program must explicitly reinitialize variables (via C-spec instructions) each time it's called.

Programs that are called repeatedly are good candidates for ending with their LR indicators set off. Because the system doesn't need to reactivate such programs or reopen any files, you'll typically experience a performance improvement if you write repeatedly called programs this way. Before ILE, when you had an application involving programs that returned with LR set off, a CL driver program would issue a RclRsc command after the call to the first RPG program to deactivate all such programs. In an ILE environment, RclRsc has no effect on programs running in named or *New activation groups. RclRsc affects only programs running in the default activation group.

But don't think that RclRsc doesn't work with ILE programs at all. In fact, RclRsc works on any program (ILE or OPM) running in the default activation group.

Moreover, RclRsc has no effect on service programs, whether they run in the default activation group or not. Service programs typically consist of RPG subprocedures running in *NoMain modules. In Chapter 3, you learned that you can't escape into the RPG cycle from an RPG subprocedure. So even if a subprocedure running in a service program sets on the LR indicator, it won't have any effect because you can't escape into the RPG cycle to have it close all files and deactivate the module. For this reason, I usually advise against running service programs in the default activation group. I'll elaborate on this advice in a moment.

Let's summarize the limitations of RclRsc in an ILE environment.

- It has no effect on programs running in named or *New activation groups.
- It has no effect on service programs, regardless of the type of activation group in which they're running.

If we're running programs in a *New activation group, we don't have to worry much about cleaning up with RclRsc because simply exiting from a *New activation group results in the activation group's deletion, thereby causing all the programs running in it to be deactivated as well. So how can we clean up programs and service programs running in named activation groups? The answer is to use the RclActGrp (Reclaim Activation Group) command.

RclActGrp, which is usually issued from a CL program, causes an activation group to be deleted. In the process, all the programs and service programs running in that activation group are deactivated. Some people refer to RclActGrp as the ILE version of the RclRsc command.

If you want to reclaim an activation group called A, you'd issue the RclActGrp command like this:

```
RclActGrp   A
```

RclActGrp must be issued from a program or from the command line running completely outside the activation group being reclaimed. To understand what I mean by *completely outside* the activation group, look at Figure 5.7.

FIGURE 5.7
RclRsc Scenarios

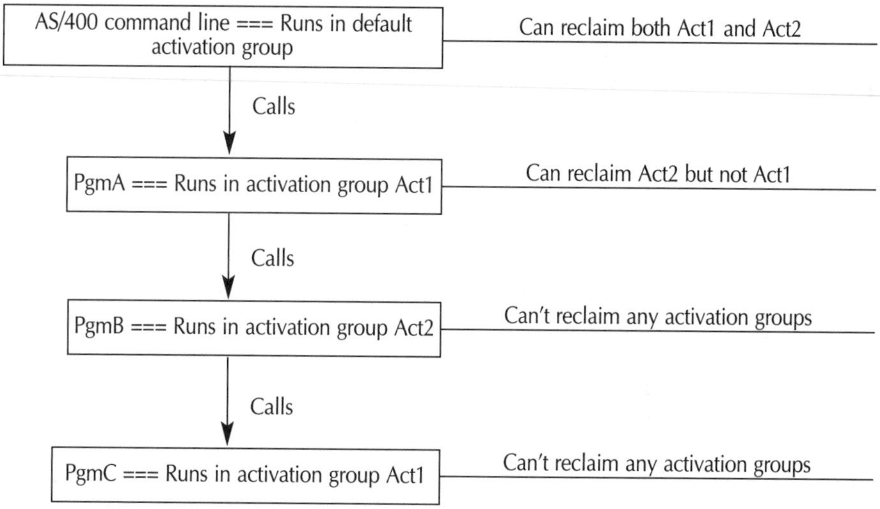

The figure shows PgmA, which is running in activation group Act1, being called from the command line, which is running in the default activation group. PgmA calls PgmB, which is running in activation group Act2. PgmB calls PgmC, which is running in Act1. As a general rule, a program can reclaim an activation group if neither itself nor any program previous to itself in the call stack is running in that activation group. (Note: You can't reclaim the default activation group.)

PgmC can't reclaim Act1 because PgmC itself and one previous program in the call stack (PgmA) are running in Act1. PgmC can't reclaim Act2 because a previous program in the call stack (PgmB) is running in Act2.

PgmB can't reclaim Act1 because a previous program in the call stack (PgmA) is running in Act1. PgmB can't reclaim Act2 because PgmB itself is running in this activation group.

PgmA can't reclaim Act1 because PgmA is running in this activation group. But PgmA can reclaim Act2 because neither itself nor any previous program in the call stack is running in Act2.

In general, the RclActGrp command will be issued from a CL driver program running in the default activation group. However, if you want an ILE RPG program to reclaim an activation group for some reason, you can use the well-known QCMDEXC API for this purpose.

RclActGrp lets you specify the special value *Eligible instead of the name of a specific activation group, but you should avoid doing this. Specifying *Eligible will delete (or reclaim) all activation groups that are eligible. You may feel you have control of what activation groups exist in your job, but you don't. Nothing stops IBM programs from creating activation groups and running some IBM software in them. I once had my interactive session terminate abnormally because I issued the command RclActGrp *Eligible.

An alternative to the RclActGrp command is the CEETREC (Normal End) API. IBM API programs are often difficult to use due to their complicated parameter structures. However, CEETREC is actually simpler to use (with respect to parameters) than the QCMDEXC API. In fact, CEETREC has no required parameters. It has two omissible parameters that I won't talk about here because they're not especially useful for our purposes. You can invoke CEETREC from an ILE RPG program as follows:

```
C                    CallB     'CEETREC'
```

CEETREC works differently than the RclActGrp command; it operates only within the activation group in which it's issued. This is roughly the opposite of RclActGrp, which operates only outside the activation group it's attempting to reclaim.

To understand how CEETREC works, you must learn some new terminology. A *control boundary* is an imaginary line drawn between two call stack entries that are running in different activation groups. A *hard control boundary* is an imaginary line between two call stack entries where the second entry is running in a different activation group from the first and is also the first call stack entry running in its own activation group.

In Figure 5.8, the four broken lines represent control boundaries. The first line is drawn between the AS/400 command line (which is running in the default activation group) and PgmA (which is running in Act1). Because PgmA is the first program running in Act1, the control boundary is labeled as a hard control boundary.

FIGURE 5.8
Control Boundary Example

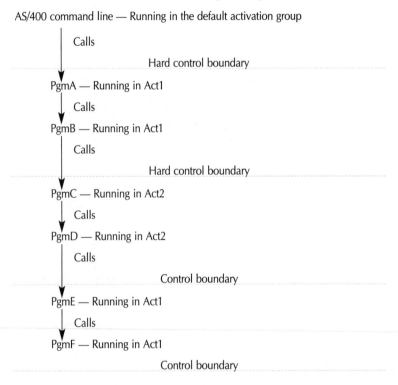

AS/400 command line — Running in the default activation group

Calls

Hard control boundary

PgmA — Running in Act1

Calls

PgmB — Running in Act1

Calls

Hard control boundary

PgmC — Running in Act2

Calls

PgmD — Running in Act2

Calls

Control boundary

PgmE — Running in Act1

Calls

PgmF — Running in Act1

Control boundary

The next control boundary is drawn between PgmB and PgmC because they run in different activation groups. This is also a hard control boundary because PgmC is the first program running in Act2.

The next control boundary is drawn between PgmD and PgmE because these two call stack entries are running in different activation groups. It's not a hard control boundary, however, because PgmE isn't the first call stack entry running in Act1. (Although it may not adhere strictly to IBM's definition of a control boundary, I've also drawn a control boundary following the final entry in the call stack (PgmF) to facilitate a simpler description of the CEETREC API's behavior.)

With these definitions in mind, let's see how CEETREC works. First, any program that issues the CEETREC API is deactivated. If a program issuing CEETREC is running in the default activation group, its deactivation is the only thing that occurs. Otherwise, CEETREC's behavior is more complicated.

When CEETREC is issued from a *New activation group, all programs running in that activation group are deactivated and the activation group is deleted. Recall that you can have more than one *New activation group running at once within a job. CEETREC affects only the *New activation group in which it's issued.

When CEETREC is issued from a program in a named activation group, its effects depend primarily on the nature of the nearest previous control boundary. If the nearest previous control boundary is a hard control boundary, the activation group is deleted and all the programs running in it are deactivated. In Figure 5.8, if CEETREC is issued from PgmA or PgmB, activation group Act1 is deleted and all the programs running in it (PgmA, PgmB, PgmE, and PgmF) are deactivated because the nearest previous control boundary is a hard control boundary. For the same reason, if CEETREC is issued from PgmC or PgmD, Act2 is deleted and PgmC and PgmD are deactivated.

When CEETREC is issued from a program running in a named activation group where the nearest previous control boundary isn't a hard control boundary, only the programs in the call stack starting from the previous control boundary to the subsequent control boundary are deactivated. In this case, the activation group isn't deleted and any call stack entries before the previous control boundary remain activated. In Figure 5.8, if CEETREC is issued from PgmE or PgmF, both these programs will be deactivated, but all previous programs (PgmA, PgmB, PgmC, and PgmD) remain activated.

Using Activation Groups with Newly Developed Applications

Before developing a new ILE RPG application, you must decide which of the three types of activation groups to use. In this section, I give you my recommendations.

I believe *New activation groups are rarely useful and sometimes harmful. The only real benefit to using *New activation groups is that programs running in them can be invoked recursively (because each invocation will run in a different *New activation group). However, this is a limited benefit because RPG subprocedures can also be invoked recursively — plus subprocedures have all the added benefits discussed in Chapter 3. So my first recommendation is to avoid, for the most part, the use of *New activation groups.

Service programs should usually run in their own named activation group that has a name different from any other named activation group used in your system (such as SrvPgmAct). Occasionally, you might decide to run a service program in *Caller if you need the program to be within the same override or commitment definition scope as the invoking program or service program. Also, if you are using data exports, the service program should run in *Caller; otherwise, the calling program won't be able to access the exported data.

ILE programs should run in either a named activation group or the default activation group. Which is best? If you have a present requirement to scope overrides or commitment control within an application, or you anticipate that you might have such a requirement in the future, you should used named activation groups. Otherwise, use the default activation group.

If you opt to use named activation groups, follow these guidelines:

- Use activation group names that are suggestive of the applications running in them, such as OrdEnt for order entry.

- Make all CL driver programs ILE CL (PDM type CLLE) programs running in the same activation group as the application in which they run. The programs should use default scoping so that all overrides and commitment definitions are scoped to the activation group in which they're running.

- Run a top-level CL program in the default activation group. Make this program an OPM CL program that presents a menu of high-level application choices to the user. The program is responsible for dispatching to the first program in a major application area and for cleaning up by issuing the appropriate RclActGrp commands after returning from that application area.

Using Activation Groups with Legacy Applications

Now let's turn to legacy applications. Here, our hands are tied for many reasons. First, if you're using third-party applications, it's usually not practical (or even possible) to use an activation group strategy different from the one used by the application provider.

Even if your legacy applications were written in house, it might not be practical for them to use anything other than the default activation group. To use a named activation group, all such programs would have to be converted to ILE RPG and ILE CL. I've heard of installations that have done this, but I've never been convinced that it was entirely necessary.

I'm assuming here that, for the most part, your legacy applications are working properly. This means that if they once had problems with scoping overrides and commitment control, those problems have been dealt with.

Does this mean you can't "plug" an ILE RPG program into a legacy system? Absolutely not. There's no reason you can't use a newly written ILE RPG program in a legacy application. You just have to be careful. If you make sure the program specifies ActGrp(*Caller), it will run in the default activation group, and it can use advanced ILE features such as subprocedures and service program calls. If you specify ActGrp(*Caller) in an ILE RPG program that's intended to be used within a legacy application, it will behave the same as other programs with respect to overrides and commitment control.

One good strategy when you need to modify an RPG/400 program is to convert it to ILE RPG (using either IBM's conversion utility CvtRpgSrc or one of several third-party products that do the same thing). So long as the converted program runs in ActGrp(*Caller), it will continue to function as before. This method also lets you use any of the advanced ILE features.

Testing Your Options

On the CD accompanying this book, I've provided the TstOvr program, which tests various override scenarios involving a mix of activation group types. The program runs several tests and creates a report showing the outcome of each test as an individual line item. This software uses two files: File1 and File2. The record format in both files consists of a single 50-character field called Field1. Figure 5.9 shows the contents of these files.

FIGURE 5.9

Contents of File1 and File2

Contents of Field1 in File1

```
This is File1, Record 01
This is File1, Record 02
This is File1, Record 03
This is File1, Record 04
This is File1, Record 05
This is File1, Record 06
This is File1, Record 07
This is File1, Record 08
This is File1, Record 09
This is File1, Record 10
This is File1, Record 11
This is File1, Record 12
This is File1, Record 13
This is File1, Record 14
This is File1, Record 15
This is File1, Record 16
This is File1, Record 17
This is File1, Record 18
This is File1, Record 19
This is File1, Record 20
```

Contents of Field1 in File2

```
This is File2, Record 01
This is File2, Record 02
This is File2, Record 03
This is File2, Record 04
This is File2, Record 05
This is File2, Record 06
This is File2, Record 07
This is File2, Record 08
This is File2, Record 09
This is File2, Record 10
This is File2, Record 11
This is File2, Record 12
This is File2, Record 13
This is File2, Record 14
This is File2, Record 15
This is File2, Record 16
This is File2, Record 17
This is File2, Record 18
This is File2, Record 19
This is File2, Record 20
```

Each test involves three programs, which we'll call Pgm1, Pgm2, and Pgm3. (The actual names of the three programs used in the test will vary depending on the test being run.) There's also a controlling program that sets up and runs each test and then invokes a program that prints the test outcome as well as records the test results to a couple of physical files. We'll discuss these reports and physical files in a moment.

In each test, Pgm1 issues an override and then reads the first record from File1. In some tests, the following override has been issued:

```
OvrDbf   File( File1 )
         ToFile( File2 )
         other-parameters
```

Obviously, in these tests, Pgm1 will read the first record from File2 due to the override. After Pgm1 reads this record, it calls Pgm2, which also reads a record. Pgm2 then calls Pgm3, which reads a record, too. In all tests, Pgm2 and Pgm3 run in the same activation group. Pgm1 can run in the same activation group as or a different one than the other two programs.

Two batteries of tests are performed. The first is a series of Share(*Yes) overrides. The second is a series of tests in which ToFile(File2) has been specified.

Figure 5.10 shows the Share Override Results Report, which details the outcome of the first series of tests run by the TstOvr software.

FIGURE 5.10

Share Override Results Report

	Iss AG Type	Subj AG Type	Override Scope	Open Scope	Same or Diff AG	Result
2/04/00 12:54:17			Share Override Results		Page 1	
	Dft	Dft	Job	Job	Same	JB
	Dft	Dft	Job	AGD	Same	JB
	Dft	Dft	AGD	Job	Same	JB
	Dft	Dft	AGD	AGD	Same	JB
	Dft	Dft	CLL	Job	Same	JB
	Dft	Dft	CLL	AGD	Same	JB
	Dft	New	Job	Job	Diff	JB
	Dft	New	Job	AGD	Diff	AG
	Dft	New	AGD	Job	Diff	JB
	Dft	New	AGD	AGD	Diff	AG
	Dft	New	CLL	Job	Diff	JB
	Dft	New	CLL	AGD	Diff	AG
	Dft	Named	Job	Job	Diff	JB
	Dft	Named	Job	AGD	Diff	AG
	Dft	Named	AGD	Job	Diff	JB
	Dft	Named	AGD	AGD	Diff	AG
	Dft	Named	CLL	Job	Diff	JB
	Dft	Named	CLL	AGD	Diff	AG
	New	Dft	Job	Job	Diff	JB
	New	Dft	Job	AGD	Diff	AG
	New	Dft	AGD	Job	Diff	NO
	New	Dft	AGD	AGD	Diff	NO
	New	Dft	CLL	Job	Diff	JB
	New	Dft	CLL	AGD	Diff	AG
	New	New	Job	Job	Same	JB
	New	New	Job	Job	Diff	JB

Ⓐ

continued

FIGURE 5.10 *CONTINUED*

Iss AG Type	Subj AG Type	Override Scope	Open Scope	Same or Diff AG	Result
New	New	Job	AGD	Same	JB
New	New	Job	AGD	Diff	AG
New	New	AGD	Job	Same	JB
New	New	AGD	Job	Diff	NO
New	New	AGD	AGD	Same	JB
New	New	AGD	AGD	Diff	NO
New	New	CLL	Job	Same	JB
New	New	CLL	Job	Diff	JB
New	New	CLL	AGD	Same	JB
New	New	CLL	AGD	Diff	AG
New	Named	Job	Job	Diff	JB
New	Named	Job	AGD	Diff	AG
New	Named	AGD	Job	Diff	NO
New	Named	AGD	AGD	Diff	NO
New	Named	CLL	Job	Diff	JB
New	Named	CLL	AGD	Diff	AG
Named	Dft	Job	Job	Diff	JB
Named	Dft	Job	AGD	Diff	AG
Named	Dft	AGD	Job	Diff	NO
Named	Dft	AGD	AGD	Diff	NO
Named	Dft	CLL	Job	Diff	JB
Named	Dft	CLL	AGD	Diff	AG
Named	New	Job	Job	Diff	JB
Named	New	Job	AGD	Diff	AG
Named	New	AGD	Job	Diff	NO
Named	New	AGD	AGD	Diff	NO
Named	New	CLL	Job	Diff	JB
Named	New	CLL	AGD	Diff	AG
Named	Named	Job	Job	Same	JB
Named	Named	Job	Job	Diff	JB
Named	Named	Job	AGD	Same	JB
Named	Named	Job	AGD	Diff	AG
Named	Named	AGD	Job	Same	JB
Named	Named	AGD	Job	Diff	NO
Named	Named	AGD	AGD	Same	JB
Named	Named	AGD	AGD	Diff	NO
Named	Named	CLL	Job	Same	JB
Named	Named	CLL	Job	Diff	JB
Named	Named	CLL	AGD	Same	JB
Named	Named	CLL	AGD	Diff	AG

Each detail line in the report represents one test. The first column (Iss AG Type) shows the activation group type that the first program (Pgm1) runs in. This column's value can be Dft (default), New, or Named. The second column (Subj AG Type) shows the activation group type in which Pgm2 and Pgm3 run. This column can have any of the same three values that the first column can have.

The next column (Override Scope) specifies what OvrScope parameter value is used in the test. This can be Job (for OvrScope(*Job)), AGD (for OvrScope(*ActGrpDfn)), or CLL (for OvrScope(*CallLvl). The next column (Open Scope) contains this information for the

OpnScope parameter. Recall, the valid OpnScope parameter values are *Job and *ActGrpDfn. Therefore, this column's value can be Job or AGD.

The next column in the report (Same or Diff AG) tells whether Pgm1 runs in the same or a different activation group than Pgm2 and Pgm3. Remember, Pgm2 and Pgm3 always run in the same activation group as each other.

The last column (Result) gives the result of the test. JB means that Pgm3 read record 3 and the open data path sharing was therefore a job-level share (at least that's how it looked to Pgm3). AG means Pgm3 read record 2 and concluded it must have been sharing only with Pgm2. NO means Pgm3 read record 1 and, therefore, must not have been sharing an open data path.

The program generates all the reasonable combinations of test setups. An example of an unreasonable combination is one in which all three programs run in the default activation group and the third also runs in a different activation group. This is impossible because only one default activation group exists within a job (other than the IBM default activation group).

Let's see whether the report of Figure 5.10 corresponds with our understanding of shared overrides' behavior. At **A** appear two of the tests in which Pgm1 runs in the default activation group and Pgm2 and Pgm3 run in a named activation group. In both tests, OvrScope(*ActGrpDfn) is used. The only difference between the two tests is that the first one uses OpnScope(*Job) and the second uses OpnScope(*ActGrpDfn). In the first test, Pgm3 reads the third record; therefore, job-level open data path sharing was used. No sharing would have occurred at all if Pgm2 and Pgm3 hadn't seen the override. Because the override was issued in the default activation group specifying OvrScope(*ActGrpDfn), it became a caller-level override and was thus seen by Pgm2 and Pgm3. Had Pgm1 run in a named or *New activation group different from that of Pgm2 and Pgm3, Pgm2 and Pgm3 wouldn't have seen the override and the Result column would have said NO, as shown by the result at **C.**

Back at **A**, notice that only activation group sharing (and not job-level sharing) was detected in the second test because the OpnScope parameter specified *ActGrpDfn. Contrast this with the first test at **A,** which used OpnScope(*Job) and resulted in job-level sharing of the open data path. Remember, the OpnScope parameter is ignored if the override isn't seen. Whether a call stack entry sees the override or not depends on the OvrScope parameter.

Two more tests appear at **B**. In both tests, all three programs run in *New activation groups and OvrScope(*ActGrpDfn) and OvrScope(*Job) are used. In the first test, all three programs are running in the same *New activation group. Because OvrScope(*ActGrpDfn) is specified, Pgm3 sees the override. Pgm2 and Pgm3 see the override only because they're running in the same activation group as Pgm1. Unlike the test at **A**, this test is issued from a *New activation group. Therefore, specifying OvrScope(*ActGrpDfn) means this override is scoped to the activation group of issue only. It can't be seen outside that activation group. Because all three programs are running in the same activation group, they share the same open data path.

The next test at **B** is the same as the first, except that Pgm2 and Pgm3 run in a different *New activation group than Pgm1. The result of no open data path sharing (i.e., Result = NO) makes sense; these programs won't see the override because it's scoped only to the activation group of issue.

The report shown in Figure 5.11 shows the results of a series of tests in which a non-share override was tested. In this case, we specified ToFile(File2).

FIGURE 5.11
Non-Share Override Results Report

```
2/04/00                    Non-Share Override Results                 Page    1
12:59:04
                 Iss AG      Subj AG    Override  Same or
                 Type        Type       Scope     Diff AG   Result
                 Dft         Dft        Job       Same      JB
                 Dft         Dft        AGD       Same      JB
                 Dft         Dft        CLL       Same      JB
                 Dft         New        Job       Diff      JB
                 Dft         New        AGD       Diff      JB
                 Dft         New        CLL       Diff      JB
                 Dft         Named      Job       Diff      JB
                 Dft         Named      AGD       Diff      JB
                 Dft         Named      CLL       Diff      JB
                 New         Dft        Job       Diff      JB
                 New         Dft        AGD       Diff      NO
                 New         Dft        CLL       Diff      JB
                 New         New        Job       Same      JB
                 New         New        Job       Diff      JB
                 New         New        AGD       Same      JB
                 New         New        AGD       Diff      NO
                 New         New        CLL       Same      JB
                 New         New        CLL       Diff      JB
                 New         Named      Job       Diff      JB
                 New         Named      AGD       Diff      NO
                 New         Named      CLL       Diff      JB
                 Named       Dft        Job       Diff      JB
                 Named       Dft        AGD       Diff      NO
                 Named       Dft        CLL       Diff      JB
                 Named       New        Job       Diff      JB
                 Named       New        AGD       Diff      NO
                 Named       New        CLL       Diff      JB
                 Named       Named      Job       Same      JB
                 Named       Named      Job       Diff      JB
     (A)         Named       Named      AGD       Same      JB
                 Named       Named      AGD       Diff      NO
                 Named       Named      CLL       Same      JB
                 Named       Named      CLL       Diff      JB
```

In this series, the third program simply tests to see whether it reads a record from File1 or File2. As Figure 5.9 shows, it can do this by simply inspecting the field of the record that it reads.

The columns in this report are the same as those of the previous report except that this report is missing the Open Scope column. (OpnScope applies only to Share(*Yes) overrides.) In the Result column, a value of JB means Pgm3 read a record from File2; a value of NO means Pgm3 read a record from File1. In these tests, we're testing only whether Pgm3 sees the override.

At **A** in Figure 5.11 appear two tests in which all three programs run in a named activation group. The first test sees the override (Result = JB) because the override is scoped to the activation group (Override Scope = AGD) and because all three programs are running in the same named activation group (i.e., Same or Diff AG = Same). The second test at **A** differs from the first only in that Pgm2 and Pgm3 run in a different named activation group from that of Pgm1 (i.e., Same or Diff Ag = Diff). This time, Pgm3 doesn't see the override because the override is narrowly scoped to the activation group of issue and because Pgm3 is running in a different activation group than the one in which the override was issued.

The TstOvr software also outputs these results into two physical files. The result of the shared override tests are placed into physical file ShrResPf. The result of the non-shared override tests are placed into file NShrResPf. Figures 5.12 and 5.13 show the DDS for these two files. You can query these files using IBM's Query/400 product, Interactive SQL, or some other query tool.

FIGURE 5.12
DDS for File ShrResPf

```
A             R RESULTREC
A               ISSAGTYPE    5              TEXT('ISSUING AG TYPE' )
A                                           COLHDG('ISSUING' 'AG' 'TYPE')
A               SUBJAGTYPE   5              TEXT('SUBJECT AG TYPE')
A                                           COLHDG('SUBJECT' 'AG' 'TYPE')
A               OVSCOPE      3              TEXT('OVERRIDE SCOPE')
A                                           COLHDG('OVR' 'SCOPE')
A               OPSCOPE      3              TEXT('OPEN SCOPE')
A                                           COLHDG('OPEN' 'SCOPE')
A               SAMEORDIFF   4              TEXT('SAME OR DIFFERENT AG')
A                                           COLHDG('SAME OR' 'DIFF AG')
A               RESULT       2              TEXT('RESULT')
A                                           COLHDG('OVERRIDE' 'DETECTED')
```

FIGURE 5.13
DDS for File NShrResPf

```
A             R RESULTREC
A               ISSAGTYPE    5              TEXT('ISSUING AG TYPE' )
A                                           COLHDG('ISSUING' 'AG' 'TYPE')
A               SUBJAGTYPE   5              TEXT('SUBJECT AG TYPE')
A                                           COLHDG('SUBJECT' 'AG' 'TYPE')
A               OVSCOPE      3              TEXT('OVERRIDE SCOPE')
A                                           COLHDG('OVR' 'SCOPE')
A               SAMEORDIFF   4              TEXT('SAME OR DIFFERENT AG')
A                                           COLHDG('SAME OR' 'DIFF AG')
A               RESULT       2              TEXT('RESULT')
A                                           COLHDG('OVERRIDE' 'DETECTED')
```

You can use the TstOvr software to test a pet theory of yours about activation groups. For example, suppose you have a theory that, for any shared override issued with the call stack participants all running the same activation group, the open data path is shared throughout the job. You could issue the following SQL statement.

```
Select   Result
  From   ShrResPf
  Where SameOrDiff = 'Same'
```

This query produces the result shown in Figure 5.14.

FIGURE 5.14

Result of Query to Test a Theory

```
OVERRIDE
DETECTED
  JB
  JB
  JB
  JB
  JB
  JB
  JB
  JB
  JB
  JB
  JB
  JB
  JB
  JB
  JB
  JB
  JB
```

Because this query specifies that Pgm3 reads record 3 in every case, your theory is true.

Summary

IBM developed activation groups to solve problems of scoping with respect to overrides and commitment control. Even if these problems don't apply to you, it's important to understand what activation groups are and how they work because it's easy to get into trouble otherwise.

There are three types of activation groups: default, named, and *New. The default activation group behaves most like OPM environments before ILE. Named activation groups provide the greatest flexibility in terms of scoping overrides and commitment control. *New activation groups are problematic because they're created whenever a program running in one is activated and they're deleted whenever the first program running in them ends. This is true even when an ILE RPG program running in a *New activation group ends with its LR indicator set off.

You can use the RclActGrp command and the CEETREC API to delete (or reclaim) activation groups. RclActGrp must be issued outside the activation group that it's attempting to reclaim. CEETREC must be issued from a program running in the activation group. The effects of CEETREC on the activation group vary depending on the nature of the nearest previous control boundary.

If you have a requirement or anticipate a future requirement for improved scoping functions, you should consider running newly developed applications in their own named activation groups. Usually, service programs should run in an activation group of their own, separate from other activation groups (unless they need to be within the same override or commitment-definition scope as their invoking programs or you are exporting data from the service program).

Converting legacy applications to run in anything but the default activation group is usually impractical. ILE RPG programs can be "plugged" into a legacy application safely if they run in activation group *Caller.

Chapter 6

ILE Exceptions and Condition Handlers

Let's begin this discussion of exceptions by considering *exception messages*. On the AS/400, a program exception is signaled by an exception message sent to an OPM program or an ILE procedure. This is usually done by the operating system in reaction to some error condition that it detects, but a user-written program can also send exception messages. For example, if the operating system determines that there was an attempt to execute a packed-decimal division by zero, it sends an escape message ("MCH1211 Attempt made to divide by zero for fixed point operation") to the failing OPM program or ILE procedure.

It's actually not precise to say that something on the AS/400 sends a message to a program or a procedure. In the AS/400 architecture, messages can be sent only to message queues, not to programs or procedures. But we say the message is sent to a program or procedure because a temporary message queue is associated with each entry on the call stack. (The message queue is temporary because it's created when the program or procedure is activated and deleted when the program or procedure is deactivated.) So when I say an ILE procedure or an OPM program receives a message, I mean that its associated message queue receives the message.

Exception Message Types

There are several types of messages, but only four of them qualify as exception messages:

- escape
- status
- notify
- function check

Escape messages are the most common and severe type. They indicate that a serious error has occurred. *Status* messages specify the status of work being done by a program or procedure. *Notify* messages are sent when a condition requires corrective action or a reply from the recipient of such messages. A *function check* is sent when all else has failed (i.e., when another type of message was sent and not handled). It results in the operating system generating an *ILE function check*, which is a special message type sent only by the system. It's an escape message with a message identifier of CEE9901. An *OPM function check* is an escape message with a message identifier of CPF9999.

Exception Handlers

When a call stack entry receives an exception message, the message may or may not be handled. In OPM, only *HLL-specific exception handlers* can be used for this purpose. For example, in RPG, a *PSSR (program status subroutine) and an INFSR (file exception/error subroutine) are HLL-specific exception handlers. Also, when using one of the arithmetic instructions (Add, Sub, Mult, Div, and Sqrt), RPG has its own specific exception handler for overflow errors.

In addition to HLL-specific exception handlers, ILE permits two other types of exception handlers: direct monitors and ILE condition handlers. *Direct monitors* are available in the C language and Java on the AS/400, and I don't cover them in detail. Suffice it to say that direct monitors can mark an exception as handled or not handled. *ILE condition handlers*, on the other hand, are available to all ILE languages, and I describe them in this chapter.

If the system detects an exception condition and an HLL-specific handler is available, the system invokes that handler and marks the exception as handled. Otherwise, if the exception occurred in an ILE procedure, the system will see whether a direct monitor or ILE condition handler is defined for the procedure. If so, the system passes control to the direct monitor or condition handler, which decides whether to handle the condition.

In all cases, if the exception is handled, normal processing resumes in the failing program or procedure at the machine (not source program) instruction following the failing instruction. If the exception isn't handled, the next course of action varies depending on whether the failing call stack entry is an OPM program or an ILE procedure.

Default Actions for Unhandled Exceptions

If an OPM program fails to handle an exception message, the system issues a CPF9999 function check message. Each OPM language behaves differently when it receives such a function check. RPG/400, for example, removes all related messages from the message queues and replaces them with its own set of messages. Other OPM languages (e.g., Cobol/400, CL) behave differently.

If an ILE program fails to handle an exception message, the message is sent to the previous call stack entry's message queue. This process is called *percolation*. When percolation occurs, exception processing continues at the previous call stack entry. Percolation continues until a control boundary is reached. (Recall that a control boundary is an imaginary line between two call stack entries running in different activation groups.) When the previous call stack entry is across a control boundary, the message is converted to a CEE9901 exception message. Figure 6.1 shows this process.

FIGURE 6.1

Unhandled Exception Default Action

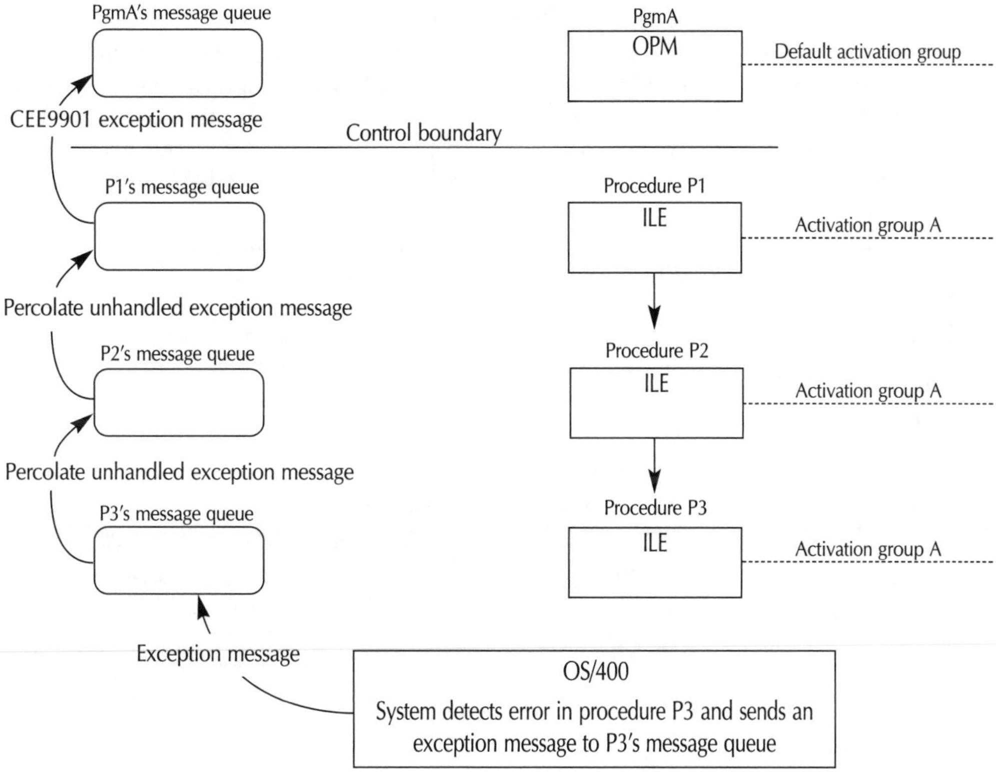

PgmA's message queue

PgmA

OPM

Default activation group

CEE9901 exception message

Control boundary

P1's message queue

Procedure P1

ILE

Activation group A

Percolate unhandled exception message

P2's message queue

Procedure P2

ILE

Activation group A

Percolate unhandled exception message

P3's message queue

Procedure P3

ILE

Activation group A

Exception message

OS/400

System detects error in procedure P3 and sends an exception message to P3's message queue

Condition Handling

ILE programs can register a condition handler procedure via the CEEHDLR (Register a User-Written Condition Handler) bindable API. This API actually sets the *handle cursor* for the procedure that invokes the API. A handle cursor is a procedure pointer maintained by the system to handle exceptions. In other words, the handle cursor (if it isn't null) points to a procedure to which the system will pass control when an exception message is sent. At that time, the system also establishes a *resume cursor*. The resume cursor is also a pointer to an executable location to resume processing if the exception is marked as "handled" by the exception-handling routine. By default, this resume cursor points to the machine instruction following the one that resulted in the exception. ILE lets you option-ally change this default via the CEEMRCR (Move Resume Cursor) bindable API.

A procedure must register its own condition handler. In particular, a procedure cannot invoke another procedure to register a condition handler on its behalf. I emphasize this because programmers often write procedures as "wrappers" for IBM APIs to simplify the tedious task of invoking them. You can't do this with the CEEHDLR bindable API because it can register a condition handler only for the procedure that invoked it.

Any ILE procedure can use CEEHDLR to register one or more procedures to handle exceptions received by that procedure. When more than one procedure is registered this way, the most recently registered procedure gets control first when an exception occurs. If that procedure decides not to handle the exception, the next most recent procedure gets control. This process continues until a condition handler marks the exception as handled or no more procedures exist to handle exceptions for the failing procedure. At this point, the exception is percolated.

A condition handler not only decides whether to handle a condition, but it also can send data to and receive data from the failing procedure. API CEEHDLR accepts a pointer to a communication area as its second parameter. This communication area can be used to communicate between the application and the condition handler.

Figure 6.2 shows the parameters used with the CEEHDLR API.

FIGURE 6.2
CEEHDLR API Parameters

	Parameter	Omissible	Type	Description
1	Condition handler	No	Procedure pointer	Points to the procedure you want to register
2	Communication area	Yes	Pointer	Points to an area of memory (usually defined in the registering procedure's data specifications) to be used as a communication area between the registering procedure and the condition handler
3	Feedback code	Yes	Data structure	Standard feedback used by CEE APIs. See Figure 6.3 for a detailed description.

Because the API is bindable, you invoke it in ILE RPG using the CallB instruction rather than the Call instruction. You can also create a prototype that lets you invoke the API with the CallP instruction.

The API's first parameter is required; it's a procedure pointer containing the address of the procedure you want to use for your condition handler.

The second parameter is a pointer to a communication area. When the condition-handling procedure receives control, this pointer is passed to it as a parameter. A failing procedure and a condition-handling procedure can communicate information to each other by placing data and inspecting data in the communication area. Although IBM documentation shows this parameter as required, it's actually omissible because if the condition-handling procedure doesn't reference the pointer, you can omit the parameter (by specifying *Omit).

The third parameter is the standard 12-byte feedback code used by most of the ILE CEE APIs. This feedback code is sometimes referred to as a *condition token*. It provides feedback to the program regarding the outcome of the API call. Figure 6.3 shows the layout of this feedback code.

FIGURE 6.3

Feedback Area Used by ILE CEE APIs

	Item	Type	Length	Description
1	Message severity	Binary	2 bytes	This is a value between 0 and 4 that corresponds roughly to the 00–99 range of AS/400 message severity.
2	Message number	Unsigned hexadecimal	2 bytes	This is the 4-digit numeric portion of the 7-character message associated with this condition. For example, suppose the message associated with this condition is CPFA08E. Then this field will contain X'A08E'. This is the hexadecimal numeric portion of the 7-character message represented in 2-byte hex format. This message number plus the Facility ID (below) form the 7-character message identifier associated with this condition.
3	Case/Severity/Control	Byte	1 byte	This is a 1-byte field broken into bit-oriented subfields. Bits 0 and 1 contain the Case field. ILE conditions are always Case 1. Bits 2–4 contain the same severity information that's contained in the Message severity field. Bits 5–7 contain a 3-bit control field that describes or controls various aspects of condition handling. The third bit specifies whether the Facility ID (below) has been assigned by IBM.
4	Facility ID	Character	3 bytes	This is actually the first three characters of a 7-character message identifier associated with this condition. For example, if the message associated with this condition is CPFA08E, the Facility ID field will contain 'CPF'. The facility ID plus the 4-digit value in the Message number field form the 7-character message associated with this condition.

Following an ILE CEE call that uses a feedback code, you can check for the call's success by inspecting the first four bytes of the feedback code. If it contains binary zeros, the API was executed successfully. Notice that by combining the information in the Message number field with the Facility ID, you can determine the AS/400 message identifier that corresponds to the failure. The 2-byte message number must be converted to a 4-byte character field before being appended to the Facility ID. Procedure pExtractMsgId (discussed later in this chapter) performs this operation.

When a procedure receives an exception message, the system passes control to the procedure registered by the CEEHDLR API. Figure 6.4 shows the parameters that are passed to this procedure.

FIGURE 6.4

Parameters Passed by the System to an ILE Condition Handler

	Item	Type	Length	Description
1	Condition token	Data structure	12 bytes	Standard 12-byte feedback code indicating the cause of the failure. See Figure 6.3 for layout.
2	Pointer to communication area	Pointer	16 bytes	This is the pointer to the communication area used by the procedure that registered this condition handler.
3	Result code	Binary	4 bytes	This is an output field set by the condition handler. Possible values are: 10 – Resume at the resume cursor 20[*]– Mark the exception as not handled 21 – Mark the exception as not handled and bypass any other condition handlers registered for the failing procedure 30 – Promote condition[†] 31 – Promote condition and bypass any other condition handlers registered for the failing procedure 32 – Promote condition and restart condition handling at the current call stack level
4	New condition	Data structure	12 bytes	Used with Result codes 30, 31, and 32, this parameter is the new condition to which the condition is promoted. If the result code is not 30, 31, or 32, this field is ignored.

[*] IBM documentation states that Result code 20 is a request to percolate the error. I consider this misleading because percolation occurs only when Result code 20 is used and no other condition handlers are registered for the failing procedure. If other condition handlers are registered, Result code 20 causes control to be transferred to the next condition handler.

[†] *Promoting a condition* means changing the condition to use a different condition. The new condition is specified in the fourth parameter.

The first parameter is a condition token that describes the problem that caused the failure. The second parameter is a pointer to a communication area. This area might contain data that was set by the failing procedure. For example, it might contain a code field instructing the condition handler to mark any condition as handled and to log the failure in a log file. This communication area can be used in a similar way to communicate information from the condition-handling procedure to the failing procedure.

The third parameter (Result code) is an output parameter that tells the system what action to take with respect to this failure. If the condition handler sets this value to 10, it's telling the system that the condition is handled and to resume processing at the resume cursor. Recall, the resume cursor usually points to the machine instruction following the failed instruction.

Setting the Result code to 20 tells the system that the condition handler elected not to handle the condition. The system will invoke the next condition handler registered for the failing procedure. If no further condition-handling procedures are registered, the system percolates the message. Note, IBM documentation describes Result code 20 as an instruction to the system to percolate the message. However, this isn't quite true. The message will be percolated only if no condition handlers remain registered for the failing procedure.

Result code 21 is the same as 20, except all further condition-handling procedures registered for the failing procedure are bypassed. Therefore, Result code 21 causes the condition to be percolated.

Result code 30 means the condition handler elected to promote the condition. *Promote* is an ILE term that means "to convert a condition to a different condition." The fourth parameter specifies the new condition. Condition processing resumes with the next condition handler registered for the failing procedure. If no further condition handler is registered, the (new) condition is percolated. Result code 31 is the same as 30, except all other registered exception handlers (if any) for the failing procedure are bypassed. Therefore, the (new) condition is percolated. Result code 32 promotes the condition and restarts condition handling for the failing procedure with the first condition handler registered for the failing procedure.

Note, the New condition parameter is used only with result codes 30, 31, and 32; it's ignored if any other result code is returned.

A Sample Condition Handler

I've written a sample application that uses a condition handler to address record-lock problems only. All other conditions will be marked as "unhandled." Figure 6.5 shows the initial screen in the TstCndHdlr application.

FIGURE 6.5

TstCndHdlr Initial Screen

```
  9/09/99              Customer Number Selection            MCRAVITZ
 13:52:43                                                   S100B54R




             Select a customer number      1



          F3=Exit










MA   a                                                      07/041
```

After the user enters a valid customer number at this screen and presses Enter, the Modify Customer Information Screen (Figure 6.6) appears.

FIGURE 6.6

TstCndHdlr Modify Customer Information Screen

```
 9/09/99              Modify Customer Information        MCRAVITZ
14:02:20                                                S100B54R


          Customer Number      1


             CUST NAME:   Wally's Widgets
               STATUS:    A
              ADDRESS:    1234 Walsh Avenue
              CUADR2:     Suite 102
                 CITY:    Lanham
                STATE:    MD
                  ZIP:    20706
              TOT DUE:        12,334.56
               REP ID:      1
        OVDUE 60 DAYS:             .00
        OVDUE 90 DAYS:             .00
             CURR DUE:        1,000.00

          F3=Exit


 A   a                                                  08/03
```

The user can modify any of the input-capable fields on this screen and then press Enter to have the TstCndHdlr software update the Customer file.

If the Customer record is locked, the user will see a window, shown in Figure 6.7, containing complete information about the locked record, including the file name, the name of the library containing the file, the member name, the record number, and the fully qualified job name that holds the lock, including the job number, user, and name.

FIGURE 6.7

TstCndHdlr Screen When Record Is Locked

```
 9/09/99              Customer Number Selection         MCRAVITZ
14:04:09                                                S100B54R



     Select a customer number      1

                   ┌──────────────────────────────────────┐
                   │         Record Locked Notification    │
                   │                                        │
                   │  This program has attempted to place a lock │
        F3=Exit    │  on a record which is already locked.  │
                   │                                        │
                   │  File:        CUST                     │
                   │  Library:     MCRAVITZ                 │
                   │  Member:      CUST                     │
                   │  Record No:      1                     │
                   │                                        │
                   │  Job:         043700/MCRAVITZ/QPADEV0004 │
                   │                                        │
                   │ Reply C to cancel or R to retry:    _  │
                   │                                        │
                   └──────────────────────────────────────┘

 A   a                                                  21/065
```

The user can retry or cancel. If the user elects to retry, the window in Figure 6.7 is redisplayed if the record is still locked. If the record isn't locked on a retry, the Modify Customer Information screen (Figure 6.6) appears. If the user elects to cancel, the initial screen (Figure 6.5) appears.

Let's see what's happening behind the scenes here. Figure 6.8 shows the source for the display file used by the condition handler service program, CondHdlr.

FIGURE 6.8

Display File CondHdlrD (Used by Service Program CondHdlr)

```
A                                      DSPSIZ(24 80 *DS3)
A        R W01
A                                      WINDOW(*DFT 15 50)
A                                      WDWBORDER((*COLOR WHT) (*DSPATR RI)-
A                                      (*CHAR '         '))
A                                    1 13'Record Locked Notification'
A                                      COLOR(WHT)
A        JOBID         28A  0 11 17COLOR(WHT)
A                                    3  3'This program has attempted to plac-
A                                      e a lock'
A                                      COLOR(WHT)
A                                    4  3'on a record that is already locke-
A                                      d.'
A                                      COLOR(WHT)
A                                   11  2'Job:'
A                                      COLOR(WHT)
A                                    6  2'File:'
A                                      COLOR(WHT)
A        FILENAME      10   0  6 17COLOR(WHT)
A                                    7  2'Library:'
A                                      COLOR(WHT)
A        FILELIB       10   0  7 17COLOR(WHT)
A                                    8  2'Member:'
A                                      COLOR(WHT)
A        MBRNAME       10   0  8 17COLOR(WHT)
A                                    9  2'Record No:'
A                                      COLOR(WHT)
A        RECNO         5Y 00  9 17COLOR(WHT)
A                                      EDTCDE(J)
A                                   13  3'Reply C to cancel or R to retry:'
A                                      DSPATR(RI)
A        SCREPLY        1   I 13 38VALUES('C' 'R')
A        R DUMMY                                                          (A)
A                                      ASSUME
A                                    3  7'x'
```

Record W01 in Figure 6.8 is the window record displayed in Figure 6.7. Notice at **A**, I've created a record called DUMMY. I never refer to this record anywhere in the CondHdlr module. It's there because it contains the ASSUME keyword, which is necessary if you want to be able to open a second display file in a job without blanking out the current display. Notice in Figure 6.7 that the non-window record in the background is still displayed behind the W01 window. This background would have been blank if I hadn't included this dummy record.

The pExtractMsgId Procedure

Now let's turn to the CondHdlr service program, shown in Figure 6.9.

FIGURE 6.9

ILE RPG Program CondHdlr (Condition Handler Service Program)

```
     H NoMain

     FCondHdlrD CF    E              WorkStn UsrOpn

(A)      * If you want to use this module, you should copy into your source
         * the lines following the "Start of copy area" comment below
         * and ending with the line preceding the "End of copy area"
         * comment line.

         *********Start of copy area***************
         * Standard types
         D MsgIdType       S             7      Based( DummyPtr )
         D  TypeNoMsgId    C                    *Blank
         D FeedbackType    S            12      Based( DummyPtr )

         * Prototypes

(B)      D pExtractMsgId   PR                   Like( MsgIdType )
         D  Feedback                            Like( FeedbackType )

(C)      D pInteractive    PR            N
         D  DummyPrm                     1      Options( *Omit )

(D)      D pCondHdlr       PR
         D  InpFeedback                         Like( FeedBackType )
         D  ActionPtr                    *
         D  ResultCode                 10I 0
         D  ResultCodeResume...
         D                 C            10
         D  ResultCodeUnhandled...
         D                 C            20
         D  NewFeedback                         Like( FeedbackType )
         *********End of copy area ***************

(E)      D HexArr          S             2      Dim(   256 )
         D                                      PerRcd( 32 )
         D                                      CtData

         * = * = * = * = * = * = * = * = * = * = * = * = * = * = * = * =
         * Procedure pInteractive - Determines whether we are running
         *                          interactively or not

         P pInteractive    B                    Export
```

continued

FIGURE 6.9 *CONTINUED*

```
D pInteractive    PI                N
D   DummyPrm                      1     Options( *Omit )

  * Local variables
D RetdInfDs        DS
D                              4
D                             10I 0 Inz( %Size( RetdInfDs ) )
D   RiJobType         61      61
D   RiTypeInteractive...
D                   C                  'I'

D LenRetdInf       S           10I 0 Inz( %Size( RetdInfDs ) )
D FmtName          S            8    Inz( 'JOBI0100' )
D QlJobName        S           26    Inz( '*' )
D IntJobId         S           16    Inz( *Blank )

C                   Call     'QUSRJOBI'
C                   Parm                 RetdInfDs
C                   Parm                 LenRetdInf
C                   Parm                 FmtName
C                   Parm                 QlJobName
C                   Parm                 IntJobId

C                   If       RiJobType = RiTypeInteractive
C                   Return   *On
C                   Else
C                   Return   *Off
C                   EndIf

P pInteractive     E

* = * = * = * = * = * = * = * = * = * = * = * = * = * = * = * =
* Procedure pExtractMsgId - Extracts the message ID from a condition
*                           token. Either returns the message ID or,
*                           if the token indicates a normal completion,
*                           returns blanks.

P pExtractMsgId    B                Export

D pExtractMsgId    PI               Like( MsgIdType )
D   Feedback                        Like( FeedbackType )

  * Local variables
D FeedbackDs       DS               Based( FeedbackDsPtr )
D   FtCondId                    4
D     FtMsgSev                  5I 0 Overlay( FtCondId       )
D     FtMsgNo                   2    Overlay( FtCondId: *Next )
D       FtMsgNoHi               1    Overlay( FtMsgNo         )
D       FtMsgNoLo               1    Overlay( FtMsgNo: *Next )
D                               1
D   FtMsgIdPrefix               3
D   FtMsgInfo                   4
```

(F)

continued

FIGURE 6.9 *CONTINUED*

(G)
```
D HexArrIdxDs      DS
D Hi2ByteBin                     5I 0
D  HiLoOrdByte                   1     Overlay( Hi2ByteBin: 2 )

D RetdMsgId        S             7
```

(H)
```
     * Set addressability to the local based feedback data structure.
C                   Eval       FeedbackDsPtr = %Addr( Feedback )
```

(I)
```
C                   If         FtCondId = *Loval
C                   Return     *Blank
C                   EndIf
```

(J)
```
     * Initialize the returned message ID with the 3-character
     * prefix.
C                   Eval       RetdMsgId = FtMsgIdPrefix

     * Convert the 2-byte hex field to external display format.
     * For example, X'E54F' is converted to the character constant
     * 'E54F'.
C                   Eval       Hi2ByteBin = *Zero
C                   Eval       HiLoOrdByte = %Subst( FtMsgNo:
C                                             1: 1    )
C                   Eval       Hi2ByteBin = Hi2ByteBin + 1
C                   Eval         %Subst( RetdMsgId: 4: 2 )
C                              = HexArr( Hi2ByteBin )

C                   Eval       Hi2ByteBin = *Zero
C                   Eval       HiLoOrdByte = %Subst( FtMsgNo:
C                                             2: 1    )
C                   Eval       Hi2ByteBin = Hi2ByteBin + 1
C                   Eval         %Subst( RetdMsgId: 6: 2 )
C                              = HexArr( Hi2ByteBin )

C                   Return     RetdMsgId

P pExtractMsgId    E

     * = * = * = * = * = * = * = * = * = * = * = * = * = * = * = * =
     * Procedure pCondHdlr - Sample condition handler. This one
     *                       handles a record-lock condition by
     *                       displaying a window if running interactively
     *                       or by sending an inquiry message to qsysopr
     *                       if not running interactively. In both
     *                       cases, the user is asked to indicate
     *                       whether they want to cancel or retry.
     *                       The user's response is then made available
     *                       to the failing procedure in the communication
     *                       area (called Action). The failing procedure
     *                       can take whatever action it wants based on
     *                       the user's response. If the failure is due to
     *                       anything other than a locked record, the
     *                       exception is marked as unhandled.
P pCondHdlr        B                      Export
```

continued

FIGURE 6.9 *CONTINUED*

```
D pCondHdlr        PI
D  InpFeedback                      Like( FeedBackType )
D  ActionPtr                   *
D  ResultCode                 10I 0
D   ResultCodeResume...
D                 C             10
D   ResultCodeUnhandled...
D                 C             20
D  NewFeedback                      Like( FeedbackType )

 * Local variables
D  Action          S          1    Based( ActionPtr )
D   ActionCncl     C               'C'
D   ActionRetry    C               'R'
D MsgId            S               Like( MsgIdType )
 * The following data structure contains the fields needed          Ⓚ
 * from the message data for IBM message CPF5027.
D MsgDtaForCPF5027...
D                 DS               Based( MsgDtaPtr )
D  MdFileName            11   20
D  MdFileLib             21   30
D  MdMbr                 31   40
D  MdRec#Area            65   68B 0
 * Note, the following overlay is defined because RPG (at least
 * during one point in its history) treated MdRec#Area as a 9-digit
 * field, thus not allowing the full range of values that can be
 * assumed in a 4-byte binary field. It might not be necessary,
 * but I made the following definition just in case.
D  MdRec#                     10I 0 Overlay( MdRec#Area )
D  MdJobId               81  108

D MsgInfDs         DS         2000                                   Ⓛ
D  MiBytesRetd                10I 0
D  MiBytesAvl                 10I 0 Inz( %Size( MsgInfDs ) )
D  MiMsgId               13   19
D  MiStartOfMsgDta...
D                        49   49

D LenMsgInf        S          10I 0 Inz( %Size( MsgInfDs ) )
D FmtName          S           8    Inz( 'RCVM0100' )
D ClStkEntry       S          10    Inz( '*' )
D ClStkCounter     S          10I 0 Inz( 2 )
D MsgType          S          10    Inz( '*NOTIFY' )
D MsgKey           S           4    Inz( *Blank )
D WaitTime         S          10I 0 Inz( *Zero )
D MsgAction        S          10    Inz( '*OLD' )

D ApiErr           DS
D  AeBytesProv               10I 0 Inz( %Size( ApiErr ) )
D  AeBytesAvl                10I 0
D  AeMsgId                7
D                         1
D  AeMsgDta             256
```

continued

FIGURE 6.9 *CONTINUED*

Ⓜ
```
      * If this is not a record timeout, mark message as unhandled.
C                       If        pExtractMsgId( InpFeedback ) <> 'RNX1218'
C                       Eval      ResultCode = ResultCodeUnhandled
C                       Return
C                       EndIf

      * Invoke the subroutine that fills in the information obtained
      * from the CPF5027 message data.
C                       ExSr      FillMsgDta

      * If the message wasn't found, mark error as unhandled.
C                       If        MsgDtaPtr = *Null
C                       Eval      ResultCode = ResultCodeUnhandled
C                       Return
C                       EndIf
```

Ⓝ
```
      * Invoke the interactive handler if running interactively; otherwise,
      * percolate this error.
C                       If        pInteractive( *Omit )
C                       ExSr      GetActionInt
C                       Else
C                       Eval      ResultCode = ResultCodeUnhandled
C                       Return
C                       EndIf

      * The following subroutine looks for the CPF5027 notify message
      * in the message queue 2 levels prior in the call stack from this
      * procedure. If it finds it, it fills in data structure
      * MsgDtaForCPF5027. If it doesn't find it, it sets the basing pointer
      * for this data structure (MsgDtaPtr) to *Null. Note, the
      * message is marked as *OLD, so that it won't be retrieved twice.
C       FillMsgDta      BegSr
```

Ⓞ
```
      * See if there is a CPF5027 message in the invoker's message queue.
C                       Call      'QMHRCVPM'
C                       Parm                MsgInfDs
C                       Parm                LenMsgInf
C                       Parm                FmtName
C                       Parm                ClStkEntry
C                       Parm                ClStkCounter
C                       Parm                MsgType
C                       Parm                MsgKey
C                       Parm                WaitTime
C                       Parm                MsgAction
C                       Parm                ApiErr
```
```
      * Set the basing pointer for data structure MsgDtaForCPF5027
      * (MsgDtaPtr) to *Null if the above call fails to find
      * a notify message CPF5027.
C                       If        AeBytesAvl > *Zero
C                       Eval      MsgDtaPtr = *Null
C                       LeaveSr
C                       EndIf
```

continued

FIGURE 6.9 *CONTINUED*

```
C                        If        MiMsgId <> 'CPF5027'
C                        Eval      MsgDtaPtr = *Null
C                        EndIf

C                        Eval      MsgDtaPtr = %Addr( MiStartOfMsgDta )

C                        EndSr

 * This subroutine displays a window to the user showing
 * the information about the file and job and record that
 * is locked. It asks the user to reply C to cancel or R to
 * retry. It places this reply into the Action field that is
 * available to the failing application procedure.
C     GetActionInt   BegSr

C                        Open      CondHdlrD


 * Fill in the output screen fields.
C                        Eval      JobId     = MdJobId
C                        Eval      FileName  = MdFileName
C                        Eval      FileLib   = MdFileLib
C                        Eval      MbrName   = MdMbr
C                        Eval      RecNo     = MdRec#

 * Get the user's reply.
C                        ExFmt     W01

 * Save the user reply in the failing procedure's supplied
 * data communication field.
C                        If        ScReply = 'R'
C                        Eval      Action    = ActionRetry
C                        Else
C                        Eval      Action    = ActionCncl
C                        EndIf

 * Specify that the exception is handled by setting a result code
 * of 10 (resume processing at the resume cursor).
C                        Eval      ResultCode = ResultCodeResume

C                        Close     CondHdlrD

C                        EndSr

 P pCondHdlr        E
```

```
**CtData HexArr
000102030405060708090A0B0C0D0E0F101112131415161718191A1B1C1D1E1F
202122232425262728292A2B2C2D2E2F303132333435363738393A3B3C3D3E3F
404142434445464748494A4B4C4D4E4F505152535455565758595A5B5C5D5E5F
606162636465666768696A6B6C6D6E6F707172737475767778797A7B7C7D7E7F
808182838485868788898A8B8C8D8E8F909192939495969798999A9B9C9D9E9F
A0A1A2A3A4A5A6A7A8A9AAABACADAEAFB0B1B2B3B4B5B6B7B8B9BABBBCBDBEBF
C0C1C2C3C4C5C6C7C8C9CACBCCCDCECFD0D1D2D3D4D5D6D7D8D9DADBDCDDDEDF
E0E1E2E3E4E5E6E7E8E9EAEBECEDEEEFF0F1F2F3F4F5F6F7F8F9FAFBFCFDFEFF
```

The comments at **A** (page 104) advise the user of this service program to copy a block of code — the "copy area" — into the using program. This copy area contains some type fields (used with the Like keyword), some named constants, and some procedure prototypes.

At **B** appears the prototype for the procedure pExtractMsgId. This procedure accepts a standard 12-byte feedback code and returns the message identifier (if any) associated with this feedback code. If the feedback code indicates a successful feedback, pExtractMsgId returns a blank message identifier.

Tip

Procedure pExtractMsgId can be useful outside the context of condition handlers. In fact, if you find yourself invoking CEE APIs that use feedback codes, you'd probably find this a very handy procedure for checking the outcome of your API calls.

At **F,** I define a based data structure consisting of the relevant parts of the 12-byte feedback code. At **H,** I set the basing pointer as the address of the feedback code that was passed as a parameter to this procedure. From this point forward, I can refer to data structure FeedbackDs and its subfields, and I'll actually be referring to the feedback code that was passed as a parameter to this procedure.

I define FtCondId as the first four bytes of the feedback code. Recall that if the first four bytes of the feedback code are binary zeros, the feedback code is the outcome of a *successful* API call. At **I,** I check FtCondId for binary zeros. If FtCondId is binary zeros, the procedure ends by returning a blank message identifier.

If control gets beyond **I** in the procedure, the feedback code has an AS/400 error message identifier encoded within it. How does the 7-character AS/400 message identifier get encoded into the feedback code? The so-called 3-byte Facility ID is actually the first three characters of this 7-character message ID. At **F,** I call this field FtMsgIdPrefix. That's easy enough. The hard part is extracting the 4-digit hexadecimal message number portion of this message identifier. This number is encoded in two bytes as unsigned hex in the Message number field. At **F,** I name this 2-byte field FtMsgNo, and I've broken it into two 1-byte fields: FtMsgNoHi and FtMsgNoLo.

The main task of the pExtractMsgId procedure is to convert this 2-byte unsigned hex field into an externally displayable 4-byte character field. To help the procedure do this, I defined a compile-time array called HexArr at **E.** Notice its dimension is 256 and each element is two characters long. Now look at the compile-time data (at the very end of the figure). The first element is a displayable "00", the second is "01", and so on. In fact, the nth element of this array is the displayable translation of $(n - 1)$ in hex format, where n may range between decimal 1 and decimal 256.

At **J,** I first initialize the return message ID (RetdMsgId) with FtMsgIdPrefix, which is the 3-character message identifier prefix. Next, I set a 2-byte binary field called Hi2ByteBin to zero. Then, I force the first two hex digits (which occupy one byte) of the message identifier into the low-order portion of this 2-byte binary field. Because RPG uses 1-origin for its arrays, I must add 1 to this value to set the proper index for my compile-time array. I then place this translated hex value into positions 4 and 5 of RetdMsgId. Below **J**, I perform a similar set of operations for the low-order byte of the FtMsgNo field, placing that result into positions 6 and 7 of the RetdMsgId. Finally, I use the ILE RPG Return statement to return this result to the caller just before the procedure end statement.

The pInteractive Procedure

At **C** in Figure 6.9 is the prototype for the pInteractive procedure, which returns an indicator variable telling whether the current job is running interactively. This variable affects how the pCondHdlr procedure (which I cover next) behaves. I made the pInteractive procedure available external to the CondHdlr service program because other programs might find it useful. The procedure uses API QUSRJOBI (Retrieve Job Information) to determine whether the current job is running interactively. Because it doesn't really pertain directly to condition handling, I don't describe this procedure in detail.

The pCondHdlr Procedure

The prototype at **D** for procedure pCondHdlr defines the parameters that the system passes to a condition handler. The first parameter (InpFeedback) is the 12-byte feedback code that describes the condition that occurred. The second parameter (ActionPtr) is a pointer to the communication area. The third parameter (ResultCode) is an output parameter that must be set by the condition handler procedure indicating the action to take (e.g., resume execution, percolate the exception). Notice, I placed two named constants (ResultCodeResume, ResultCodeUnhandled) as possible values this output field may assume. There are several other possible output values, but these two are the ones used by this procedure. The fourth parameter (NewFeedback) is the feedback code used when promoting a condition. Because pCondHdlr doesn't engage in condition promoting, the parameter is unused by this procedure.

Now look at the based field called Action (just before **K** in the figure). Notice that it's based on ActionPtr, which is the pointer to the communication area passed as the second parameter to procedure pCondHdlr. The two named constants (ActionCncl and ActionRetry) contain the possible values ('C' and 'R') the user may use to reply to this error message.

At **K** I've defined a based data structure called MsgDtaForCPF5027. Although ILE RPG issues an RNX1218 escape message when a record-lock condition occurs, ILE RPG actually does this in reaction to the notify message CPF5027, which is issued by the system. Message CPF5027 contains important message data regarding the locked record, including the file name and library as well as the job that holds the lock. The fact that ILE RPG issues message RNX1218 is unique to RPG. Other languages behave differently. This condition handler is set to work only for record locks occurring in an ILE RPG program.

Data structure MsgDtaForCPF5027 (at **K**) contains subfields of AS/400 message CPF5027's message data used by this subprocedure. For example, positions 11–20 of this message data contain the file name for the record lock.

Okay, let's look at the executable code! At **M**, I check to see whether this is a record-lock exception. I use the pExtractMsgId procedure to determine whether the 12-byte condition code is for message 'RNX1218'. If not, the failure is something other than a record lock and the condition is marked as unhandled.

Next, subroutine FillMsgDta is invoked to obtain the important message data contained in the notify message CPF5027. The main job of this subroutine is to set the basing pointer (MsgDtaPtr) for the MsgDtaForCPF5027 data structure to point to the actual CPF5027 message data. It sets MsgDtaPtr to *Null if it's unable to do this for any reason. I'll cover this subroutine in detail in a moment. But first, notice that following the ExSr operation on subroutine FillMsgDta, the procedure tests the pointer MsgDtaPtr for *Null. If the pointer is null, the condition is marked as unhandled.

Now look at **N** in the figure. Control is passed to this point in the procedure if the FillMsgDta subroutine successfully locates the CPF5027 message data. The pInteractive procedure is used to determine whether the job is running interactively. If so, the procedure invokes subroutine GetActionInt to display the window in Figure 6.7 to determine whether the user wants to cancel or retry. If the job isn't running interactively, the procedure marks the condition as unhandled.

Just after **N,** subroutine FillMsgDta uses message-handling API QMHRCVPM (Receive Program Message) at **O** to retrieve the CPF5027 message. This API populates a predefined data structure that I called MsgInfDs (defined at **L**). Although the API populates this data structure with a large amount of information regarding the retrieved message, I've defined only those subfields necessary for this procedure's purposes. The most important of these subfields is MiStartOfMsgDta, which marks the beginning of the message data that's returned by API QMHRCVPM.

After the API call at **O**, FillMsgDta tests the bytes available field (AeBytesAvl) of the standard API error data structure (ApiErr). This field will be zero if the API successfully retrieved a message. Note, the subroutine sets the MsgDtaPtr to *Null if the API fails. Next, it sets MsgDtaPtr to *Null if it didn't find the CPF5027 message. Otherwise, it sets MsgDtaPtr to point to the beginning of the message data area returned by the API.

Now look at the GetActionInt subroutine at **P**. In the F-spec (near the beginning of Figure 6.9) for display file CondHdlrD, I used the UsrOpn keyword because CondHdlr is run as a service program. Because CondHdlr is a NoMain module (see the H-spec at the beginning of the figure) and will be placed into a service program, there's no way to deactivate it without reclaiming the activation group in which it's running. It is therefore cleaner to open and close the file explicitly. Notice that the first and last instructions in subroutine GetActionInt open and close the file.

After opening the display file, the subroutine moves (via the five Eval statements) the locked-record description information from the CPF5027 message data area to similar fields defined in the screen record. Next, it uses the ExFmt instruction to display the window to the user. Next, the user's response is transferred to the Action communication area so the failing procedure can take the appropriate action.

The Eval statement just before the Close statement marks the condition as handled, which results in the system returning control to the instruction following the failing instruction. Note, the system actually returns control to the *machine instruction* (not the source instruction) following the failed instruction. In this case, control eventually and harmlessly passes to the machine instruction corresponding to the start of the next source instruction. So it works well here. In fact, it works well in the majority of cases. But you need to be aware that the resume cursor is set (by default) to the machine instruction (not the source instruction) following the failed instruction. You should carefully test your condition handler to see whether this is adequate in your situation.

Figure 6.10 shows the source for program TstCndHdlr. TstCndHdlr has an input file called Cust whose DDS is shown in Figure 6.11.

FIGURE 6.10
ILE RPG Program TstCndHdlr

```
FCust        UF   E           K Disk                                      Ⓐ
FTstDspf     CF   E             WorkStn

 * Standard types
D MsgIdType        S             7         Based( DummyPtr )
D  TypeNoMsgId     C                       *Blank
D FeedbackType     S            12         Based( DummyPtr )

 * Prototypes

D pExtractMsgId    PR                      Like( MsgIdType )
D  Feedback                               Like( FeedbackType )

D pInteractive     PR            N
D  DummyPrm                      1         Options( *Omit )

D pCondHdlr        PR
D  InpFeedback                            Like( FeedBackType )
D  ActionPtr                     *
D  ResultCode                  10I 0
D   ResultCodeResume...
D                  C            10
D   ResultCodeUnhandled...
D                  C            20
D  NewFeedback                            Like( FeedbackType )

D MyProcPtr        S             *         ProcPtr                        Ⓑ
D                                          Inz( %Paddr( 'PCONDHDLR' ) )

D Feedback         S                       Like( FeedbackType )
D RetdMsgId        S                       Like( MsgIdType )
D DummyVar         S             1
D Action           S             1                                        Ⓒ
D  ActionRetry     C                       'R'
D  ActionCancel    C                       'C'
D ActionPtr        S             *         Inz( %Addr( Action ) )
```

continued

FIGURE 6.10 *CONTINUED*

```
D IndDsPtr          S              *    Inz( %Addr( *IN ) )
D IndDs             DS                  Based( IndDsPtr )
D   ExitPgm                3     3N
D   RecordNotFound...
D                         99    99N
```

```
* Register the demo condition handler. Note, this particular handler
* communicates back to the application through a single 1-byte field.
* The field contains a value of 'R' (for retry) if the user wants
* to retry the operation or 'C' if the user wants to cancel.
C                   CallB     'CEEHDLR'
C                   Parm                    MyProcPtr
C                   Parm                    ActionPtr
C                   Parm                    FeedBack
```

```
* Get the error message associated with the FeedBack area
* (if any). To do this, I invoke the pExtractMsgId procedure
* provided in the CondHdlr service program.
C                   Eval      RetdMsgId = pExtractMsgId( FeedBack )
C                   If        RetdMsgId <> *Blank
C     'Reg. Failed' Dsply                   DummyVar
C                   Eval      *INLR = *On
C                   Return
C                   EndIf
```

```
C                   DoU       ExitPgm

C                   ExFmt     R01

C                   If        ExitPgm
C                   Leave
C                   EndIf

C                   ExSr      GetCustRec

C                   If        RecordNotFound
C                   Iter
C                   EndIf

C                   ExFmt     R02
C                   Update    CusRec

C                   If        ExitPgm
C                   Leave
C                   EndIf

C                   EndDo

C                   Eval      *INLR = *On
```

```
* This subroutine retrieves the customer record. It is sensitive to
* the possibility that the record might be locked. It determines
* whether the user wants to retry or cancel by inspecting the
* Action field. Note that this field is used to communicate between
* the condition handler and this procedure.
C     GetCustRec    BegSr
```

continued

FIGURE 6.10 *CONTINUED*

```
C                     DoU         Action = *Blank                          (H)
C                                 Or Action = ActionCancel
C                     Eval        Action = *Blank

C         CuNum       Chain       Cust

C                     If          Action = ActionRetry
C                     Iter
C                     EndIf

* Set on error message indicator if record is not found.
C                     If          %Found
C                     Eval        RecordNotFound = *Off
C                     Else
C                     Eval        RecordNotFound = *On
C                     EndIf

C                     EndDo

C                     EndSr
```

FIGURE 6.11

DDS for Physical File Cust

```
A                                       UNIQUE
A           R CUSREC
A             CUNUM         3S 0        TEXT('CUSTOMER NUMBER')
A                                       COLHDG('CUST NO.')
A             CUNAME        25          TEXT('CUSTOMER NAME')
A                                       COLHDG('CUST' 'NAME')
A             CUSTAT        1           TEXT('STATUS, A=ACTIVE, I=INACTIVE')
A                                       COLHDG('STATUS')
A             CUADR1        25          TEXT('ADDRESS LINE 1')
A                                       COLHDG('ADDRESS')
A             CUADR2        25          TEXT('ADDRESS LINE 2')
A             CUCITY        20          TEXT('CITY')
A                                       COLHDG('CITY')
A             CUSTTE        2           TEXT('STATE')
A                                       COLHDG('STATE')
A             CUZIP         9           TEXT('ZIP CODE')
A                                       COLHDG('ZIP')
A             CUTOTD        9S 2        TEXT('TOTAL AMOUNT DUE')
A                                       COLHDG('TOT DUE')
A             CUCURD        9S 2        TEXT('CURRENT AMOUNT DUE')
A                                       COLHDG('CURR DUE')
A             CUREP         3S 0        TEXT('SALES REP ID')
A                                       COLHDG('REP ID')
A             CUOV30        9S 2        TEXT('OVERDUE 30 DAYS AMOUNT')
A                                       COLHDG('OVDUE' '30 DAYS')
A             CUOV60        9S 2        TEXT('OVERDUE 60 DAYS AMOUNT')
A                                       COLHDG('OVDUE' '60 DAYS')
A             CUOV90        9S 2        TEXT('OVERDUE 90 DAYS AMOUNT')
A                                       COLHDG('OVDUE' '90 DAYS')
A           K CUNUM
```

At **A** in Figure 6.10 appears the copy area, which was copied from the copy area in the CondHdlr source module. At **B**, I define a procedure pointer called MyProcPtr. I use the Inz keyword to initialize this procedure pointer to the address of the pCondHdlr procedure. Notice that even though RPG is case insensitive, I must specify the name of pCondHdlr in all upper case here because the argument of the %Paddr built-in function must be a character constant and 'PCONDHDLR' is the actual name of the pCondHdlr procedure.

At **C** I define the 1-byte Action communication area that I'll use to communicate information between the condition handler and this procedure. This Action field will actually hold the user's response (R to retry or C to cancel) to the window displayed by the condition handler. For this reason, I define the named constants ActionRetry and ActionCancel, which contain the values R and C, respectively. Notice I also define a standalone pointer field called ActionPtr, which is initialized to contain the address of the Action field. I do this because API CEEHDLR insists that I pass a pointer to the communication area and not the communication area itself.

The odd-looking data structure defined at **D** (IndDs) is based on a pointer field (IndDsPtr) that's defined and initialized on the source line just preceding the IndDs definition. I initialize the IndDsPtr pointer field to the address of this module's 99-indicator array (*IN). Therefore, the subfield RecordNotFound, which is defined to be a 1-byte field in position 99 of this data structure, is actually indicator 99. Notice in Figure 6.12 (which shows the TstDspf display file DDS) that the error message is conditioned with indicator 99 (at **A**). Therefore, if the program sets the field RecordNotFound to *On, the error message will be displayed.

FIGURE 6.12

DDS for Display File TstDspf

```
A                                         DSPSIZ(24 80 *DS3)
A            R R01
A                                         CF03(03)
A                                    1  4DATE
A                                         EDTCDE(Y)
A                                         COLOR(WHT)
A                                    2  4TIME
A                                         COLOR(WHT)
A                                    1 68USER
A                                         COLOR(WHT)
A                                    2 68SYSNAME
A                                         COLOR(WHT)
A                                    1 28'Customer Number Selection'
A                                         COLOR(WHT)
A                                    7 13'Select a customer number'
A            CUNUM     R      B      7 41REFFLD(CUSREC/CUNUM *LIBL/CUST)
A                                         EDTCDE(Z)
A    99                              10 14'Customer not found.'
A                                         COLOR(RED)
A                                         DSPATR(RI)
```

Ⓐ is marked at the line `A    99    10 14'Customer not found.'`

continued

FIGURE 6.12 *CONTINUED*

```
A                                          12 15'F3=Exit'
A                                             COLOR(BLU)
A             R R02                           CF03(03)
A                                           1  4DATE
A                                             EDTCDE(Y)
A                                             COLOR(WHT)
A                                           2  4TIME
A                                             COLOR(WHT)
A                                           1 68USER
A                                             COLOR(WHT)
A                                           2 68SYSNAME
A                                             COLOR(WHT)
A                                           1 28'Modify Customer Information'
A                                             COLOR(WHT)
A                                           5 18'Customer Number'
A             CUNUM     R       O           5 36REFFLD(CUSREC/CUNUM *LIBL/CUST)
A                                             EDTCDE(Z)
A                                           8 19'CUST NAME:'
A             CUNAME    R       B           8 31REFFLD(CUSREC/CUNAME *LIBL/CUST)
A                                           9 22'STATUS:'
A             CUSTAT    R       B           9 31REFFLD(CUSREC/CUSTAT *LIBL/CUST)
A                                          10 21'ADDRESS:'
A             CUADR1    R       B          10 31REFFLD(CUSREC/CUADR1 *LIBL/CUST)
A                                          11 22'CUADR2:'
A             CUADR2    R       B          11 31REFFLD(CUSREC/CUADR2 *LIBL/CUST)
A                                          12 24'CITY:'
A             CUCITY    R       B          12 31REFFLD(CUSREC/CUCITY *LIBL/CUST)
A                                          13 23'STATE:'
A             CUSTTE    R       B          13 31REFFLD(CUSREC/CUSTTE *LIBL/CUST)
A                                          14 25'ZIP:'
A             CUZIP     R       B          14 31REFFLD(CUSREC/CUZIP *LIBL/CUST)
A                                          15 21'TOT DUE:'
A             CUTOTD    R       B          15 31REFFLD(CUSREC/CUTOTD *LIBL/CUST)
A                                             EDTCDE(J)
A                                          16 22'REP ID:'
A             CUREP     R       B          16 31REFFLD(CUSREC/CUREP *LIBL/CUST)
A                                             EDTCDE(Z)
A                                          17 15'OVDUE 60 DAYS:'
A             CUOV60    R       B          17 31REFFLD(CUSREC/CUOV60 *LIBL/CUST)
A                                             EDTCDE(J)
A                                          18 15'OVDUE 90 DAYS:'
A             CUOV90    R       B          18 31REFFLD(CUSREC/CUOV90 *LIBL/CUST)
A                                             EDTCDE(J)
A                                          19 20'CURR DUE:'
A             CUCURD    R       B          19 31REFFLD(CUSREC/CUCURD *LIBL/CUST)
A                                             EDTCDE(J)
A                                          21 18'F3=Exit'
A                                             COLOR(BLU)
```

Finally, notice also at **D** in Figure 6.10 that I've given the name ExitPgm to indicator 3.

At **E** in Figure 6.10, I register procedure pCondHdlr as the condition handler used by this procedure. The CEEHDLR API takes three parameters (see Figure 6.2). The first (MyProcPtr) is the procedure pointer that was initialized to contain the address of procedure pCondHdlr. This tells the API which procedure is being registered as the condition handler. The second parameter (ActionPtr) is a pointer to the communication area. The third and final parameter (FeedBack) is the standard 12-byte feedback code used by many CEE APIs (and discussed earlier in this chapter).

At **F**, I use the pExtractMsgId procedure to help me check for the success of the CEEHDLR API call. Recall that this procedure will return blank if no error message is associated with the feedback code. Also at **F**, I test this returned message ID for blank. If it's not blank, I assume the call failed, display an error message, and quit.

At **G** is a standard screen-record-handling loop. This loop continues until the user presses the F3 key to quit. After displaying the screen record (R01) asking for the customer number, the program invokes the subroutine GetCustRec, which attempts to retrieve this customer record.

Before we examine subroutine GetCustRec, note that the loop tests the indicator variable called RecordNotFound to see whether the invoking routine successfully retrieved the customer record. If RecordNotFound is *On, the loop routine simply iterates displaying R01 again, only with the error message. If RecordNotFound is *Off, the loop routine continues by presenting the update screen (R02), which lets the user make record changes. When control returns, the record is updated. Following both ExFmt instructions in the loop, the user can press the F3 key. If the user presses F3 (or the ExitPgm key, as it's called here) at either point, the main loop terminates with a Leave instruction, causing the program to end.

Now let's talk about the GetCustRec subroutine, at **H**. This subroutine tries to use the RPG Chain instruction to obtain the requested customer record. It might seem odd that chaining a record requires a Do loop, as shown. The reason for this is the potential record-locked situation. The loop begins by initializing the Action communication area to a value of *Blank. Next appears the Chain instruction.

After the Chain instruction, the Action area is inspected. The only reason why this Action field would no longer be blank is if the Chain failed and the registered condition handler therefore changed the Action field. If the field's value is ActionRetry, it means the user entered a value of 'R' (for retry) at the record-lock information window. In this case, the Iter instruction ensures the Chain instruction will be retried.

If the user enters 'C' to cancel, the cancel action occurs automatically because the subsequent test of the built-in function %Found will result in the RecordNotFound (or indicator 99) field set to *On. Remember from the main loop that the system will simply redisplay the original record (R01). If the condition handler was never invoked, the test for record found results in the proper action taking place. So no explicit test to see whether the Action field equals ActionCancel is necessary.

Ways You Can Improve This Condition Handler

You can use my sample condition handler with any interactive ILE RPG program that attempts to retrieve records in update mode (thus locking the records). However, I intended it to be suggestive and not necessarily a complete handler that satisfies all your shop's needs. Although you may find the procedure useful as written, you might do several things to make it more useful. Here are a few ideas.

This condition handler will operate properly only on record locks in ILE RPG. Through experimentation, you can discover other ILE languages' behavior with respect to record locks. You could easily use this information to augment the pCondHdlr procedure to address locks in these other languages as well.

Also, the condition handler handles lock conditions only for interactive jobs. You might add a subroutine to handle cases in which the job isn't running interactively. For example, if your installation has a full-time operator that monitors the QSYSOPR message queue, you might decide to send an inquiry message to the QSYSOPR message queue asking the operator to reply 'R' to retry or 'C' to cancel.

Finally, this condition handler handles only record locks. You might decide to augment it to handle other types of errors as well.

Summary

When the system detects a user program failure, it sends an exception message to the failing program. The failing program may or may not handle the exception. If the program handles the exception, the system ignores the exception. If the program fails to handle the exception, the system either percolates the exception (for ILE procedures) or issues a function check (for OPM programs). ILE procedures that lie at a control boundary and don't handle the exception will result in an ILE function check (escape message CEE9901).

An ILE procedure may use the CEEHDLR API to register a condition handler. When an ILE procedure has registered a procedure to act as a condition handler, the handler can indicate to the system whether it chose to handle the condition or not. If the handler elects to handle the condition, the system returns control to the machine instruction following the failing instruction upon completion of the condition-handling procedure. This design is generally far superior to the INFSR and *PSSR subroutines' capability in ILE RPG because these subroutines can return control only to various points within the RPG cycle.

Chapter 7

Cancel Handlers: A Well-Kept Secret

Now I'll describe one of the best-kept secrets about ILE: *cancel handlers*, which have been available since OS/400 V2R3. If you register a cancel handler procedure in your ILE RPG program, it automatically receives control if the program is canceled for any reason.

For example, imagine your batch-update program is in the middle of a process that shouldn't be interrupted, but someone with enough authority (such as an operator) decides to cancel your program with the EndJob command. Your error-handling routines never receive control. However, your program could register a cancel handler to output enough information to a control file to let you restart the process where it left off.

Or say you want to set up a never-ending batch program that performs some crucial function, such as inventory management. You could include the program as an autostart job (so it starts whenever the subsystem starts) and then register a cancel handler that submits a job to batch invoking this same program. This way, if the job is canceled for any reason, the program is automatically restarted.

The NEP Program

The NEP program (available on your CD) shows how you can use a cancel handler. This program basically does nothing, but it represents a program running in batch that waits for a message to arrive in either a data queue or a message queue. The NEP program suspends itself for 60 seconds by passing the DlyJob (Delay Job) command to IBM's QCMDEXC API. After 60 seconds, the program loops back and executes the DlyJob command again. It continues this way until somebody or something cancels the job.

When the job is canceled, the system automatically passes control to NEP's cancel handler procedure (which NEP has previously registered). The cancel handler checks a data area called Action. If this 1-byte data area contains the value 'q' or 'Q' (for quit), the cancel handler lets the job end. If the data area doesn't contain one of these values, the cancel handler submits a similar job (running the NEP program) to batch.

I'm assuming that NEP must be running at all times. The idea is that if someone cancels the NEP job, it must be a mistake, so the program submits itself to batch to be run again. Of course, you must have some way to cancel the job for good, so I included the Action data area mechanism. If someone really needs to cancel NEP, they must first set the Action data area to a value of 'q' or 'Q'. This design lets you cancel NEP if you really need to but discourages accidental or frivolous cancellation.

How NEP Works Internally

Figure 7.1 shows the source for the NEP program. At **B**, I call the CEERTX (Register Cancel Handler) API to register the cancel handler procedure.

FIGURE 7.1
ILE RPG Program NEP

```
* Standard types
D MsgIdType       S              7     Based( DummyPtr )
D FeedbackType    S             12     Based( DummyPtr )

* Prototypes

D pExtractMsgId   PR                   Like( MsgIdType )
D  Feedback                            Like( FeedbackType )

D pCnclHdlr       PR
D  OptionalPtr                   *     Options( *Omit )
D                                      Const

D As400Cmd        PR                   ExtPgm( 'QCMDEXC' )
D  Cmd                         500     Const
D  LenCmd                     15P 5    Const

* Other data
```

Ⓐ
```
D MyProcPtr       S              *     ProcPtr
D                                      Inz( %Paddr( 'PCNCLHDLR' ) )
D FeedbackMsg     S             50
D Feedback        S                    Like( FeedbackType )
D MsgId           S                    Like( MsgIdType )
D DummyVar        S              1
D EndedMsg        C                    'Program Ended'
D DlyJob          C                    'DlyJob 60'
D Forever         S              N     Inz( *On )
D ActionDtaAra    S              1     DtaAra( ACTION )
```

Ⓑ
```
* Register pCnclHdlr as this program's cancel handler.
C                   CallB     'CEERTX'
C                   Parm                    MyProcPtr
C                   Parm                    *Omit
C                   Parm                    Feedback
```

Ⓒ
```
* If we get a negative feedback, then end this program.
C                   Eval      MsgId = pExtractMsgId( Feedback )
C                   If        MsgId <> *Blank
C                   Eval      FeedbackMsg =   'CEERTX returned '
C                                           + MsgId
C     FeedbackMsg   Dsply
C     EndedMsg      Dsply                   DummyVar
C                   Eval      *INLR = *On
C                   Return
C                   EndIf
```

Ⓓ
```
* Loop harmlessly forever. When operator cancels this program,
* cancel handler takes over. If you really want this program
* to end, then place a 'Q' into your ACTION data area.
C                   DoW       Forever
C                   CallP     As400Cmd( DlyJob: %Size( DlyJob ) )
C                   EndDo
```

continued

FIGURE 7.1 *CONTINUED*

```
* = * = * = * = * = * = * = * = * = * = * = * = * = * = * = * = * =   Ⓔ
* pCnclHdlr - Cancel handler. This routine checks the contents of
*             a 1-byte data area called Action. If Action does not
*             contain a value of 'Q' or 'q' (for quit), the program
*             resubmits itself to batch, thus making it difficult
*             to cancel this particular program.
P pCnclHdlr        B

D pCnclHdlr        PI
D  OptionalPtr                     *    Options( *Omit )
D                                       Const
 * Local data definitions
D SbmJob           C                    'SbmJob Job( NEP ) +
D                                       Cmd( Call NEP )'

 * Retrieve current contents of the ACTION data area
C                  In        ActionDtaAra

 * If the Action data area is not 'Q' or 'q' (for quit) then
 * resubmit this job
C                  If        ActionDtaAra <> 'Q'
C                  And ActionDtaAra <> 'q'
C                  CallP     As400Cmd( SbmJob: %Size( SbmJob ) )
C                  EndIf

P pCnclHdlr        E
```

Figure 7.2 shows the parameters used by API CEERTX.

FIGURE 7.2

Parameters for API CEERTX

	Parameter	Omissible	Type	Description
1	Cancel handler	No	Procedure pointer	Points to the procedure you want to register
2	Communication area	Yes	Pointer	Points to an area of memory (usually defined in the registering procedure's D-specs) to be used as a communication area between the registering procedure and the cancel handler
3	Feedback code	Yes	Data structure	Standard feedback used by CEE APIs. See Figure 6.3 (page 99) for a detailed description.

The first parameter is required and must be a procedure pointer that contains the address of the procedure you want to use as your cancel handler. The second parameter is omissible. If it's not omitted, it must be a pointer to a communication area. This is analogous to the communication area you use when registering condition handlers with the CEEHDLR API, as described in Chapter 6. The third parameter is also omissible; it's the standard 12-byte feedback code used by most of the CEE APIs (shown in Figure 6.3, page 99, in Chapter 6).

Figure 7.3 shows the parameter received by cancel handlers.

FIGURE 7.3

Parameter Passed by the System to a Cancel Handler

Item	Type	Length	Description
1 Pointer to communication area	Pointer	16 bytes	This is the pointer to the communication area used by the procedure that registered this cancel handler. This pointer will contain *Null if the communication area was specified as *Omit when the cancel handler was registered.

Notice that there's only one (omissible) parameter, a pointer to the communication area. As the description states, if you omit the parameter (by specifying *Omit), the pointer is set to *Null. A cancel handler can check to see whether a communication area pointer was passed to it by checking whether the pointer is equal to *Null.

At **B** in Figure 7.1, I have coded MyProcPtr as the first parameter passed to CEERTX. Notice at **A**, I initialize this procedure pointer with the address of pCnclHdlr. I must use all upper case in the %Paddr built-in function argument because 'PCNCLHDLR' is the actual name of the procedure. Because the argument is expressed as a character constant, RPG won't convert lower case to upper case.

The second parameter passed at **B** is *Omit. This is the omissible communication area. I elected not to pass anything for this parameter. Later in this chapter, I'll show how to use this communication area.

The final parameter passed to the CEERTX API at **B** is the standard 12-byte feedback code. At **C**, this feedback code is tested with the help of the pExtractMsgId procedure, which I exported from the CondHdlr service program discussed in Chapter 6. The do-nothing-forever loop, which I alluded to earlier, appears at **D**.

Now look at **E**, where the pCnclHdlr procedure is coded. This procedure is the actual cancel handler. After it's registered at **B**, it receives control automatically whenever this program is canceled for any reason.

The first C-spec in this procedure uses the In opcode to retrieve the contents of the Action data area. Next, if the Action data area isn't equal to 'q' or 'Q', the procedure uses the prototyped QCMDEXC API to submit a job to batch that re-invokes the NEP program. Then the cancel-handling procedure ends, which results in the original NEP job ending. However, a new one has been started if the Action data area doesn't contain 'q' or 'Q'.

What If My Cancel Handler Fails?

In the NEP example, if somebody changes the library list so that the cancel handler can't find the Action data area, the cancel handler will abnormally terminate. In this case, the system cancels the process to prevent an infinite loop of cancel handlers.

A Not-So-Simple Example

In the NEP program of Figure 7.1, the cancel handler resides in the same source as the registering procedure, so it has access to global data (data defined in the main procedure).

At **E** in Figure 7.1, pCnclHdlr takes advantage of this by referencing the data area ActionDtaAra. If I put the cancel handler into a different module that's either bound by copy into the program or bound by reference into a service program, the data that's global to procedures within the main module isn't available to the cancel handler. I could use the Export keyword in the main module and the Import keyword in the cancel handler to gain access to this data. But as a general rule of thumb, it isn't a good practice to make data available to other modules this way because it's easy to produce unforeseen side effects.

There's another way to do this, however. You can write a cancel handler that exists in a different module than the underlying application and yet has access to selected data in the canceled module. In fact, you might want to place a general-purpose cancel handler in a service program so any ILE program can use it.

Figures 7.4 and 7.5 show a variation of the NEP program split into two modules: NEP1 and NEP2. NEP1 contains the pseudo-application logic. NEP2 is the source for a service program that contains the pCnclHdlr procedure.

FIGURE 7.4
ILE RPG Program NEP1

```
 * Standard types
D MsgIdType       S              7         Based( DummyPtr )
D FeedbackType    S             12         Based( DummyPtr )

 * Prototypes

D pExtractMsgId   PR                       Like( MsgIdType )
D   Feedback                              Like( FeedbackType )

D pCnclHdlr       PR
D   OptionalPtr                  *         Options( *Omit )
D                                          Const

D As400Cmd        PR                       ExtPgm( 'QCMDEXC' )
D   Cmd                        500         Const
D   LenCmd                     15P 5 Const

 * Other data
D MyProcPtr       S              *         ProcPtr
D                                          Inz( %Paddr( 'PCNCLHDLR' ) )
D FeedbackMsg     S             50
D Feedback        S                        Like( FeedbackType )
D MsgId           S                        Like( MsgIdType )
D DummyVar        S              1
D EndedMsg        C                        'Program Ended'
D DlyJob          C                        'DlyJob 10'                    (A)
D Forever         S              N         Inz( *On )
D ActionDtaAra    S              1         DtaAra( ACTION )
D ActionPtr       S              *         Inz( %Addr( ActionDtaAra ) )   (B)
```

continued

FIGURE 7.4 CONTINUED

(C)

```
* Register pCnclHdlr as this program's cancel handler.
C                   CallB     'CEERTX'
C                   Parm                    MyProcPtr
C                   Parm                    ActionPtr
C                   Parm                    Feedback

* If we get a negative feedback, then end this program.
C                   Eval      MsgId = pExtractMsgId( Feedback )
C                   If        MsgId <> *Blank
C                   Eval      FeedbackMsg =   'CEERTX returned '
C                                           + MsgId
C    FeedbackMsg    Dsply
C    EndedMsg       Dsply                   DummyVar
C                   Eval      *INLR = *On
C                   Return
C                   EndIf
```

(D)

```
* Loop harmlessly forever. When operator cancels this program,
* cancel handler takes over. If you really want this program
* to end, then place a 'Q' or 'q' into your ACTION data area.
C                   DoW       Forever

* Set up the ActionDtaAra with the current contents of the data area.
C                   In        ActionDtaAra

C                   CallP     As400Cmd( DlyJob: %Size( DlyJob ) )
C                   EndDo
```

FIGURE 7.5

ILE RPG Service Program NEP2

```
H NoMain

D pCnclHdlr       PR
D  OptionalPtr                    *    Options( *Omit )

D                                      Const

* = * = * = * = * = * = * = * = * = * = * = * = * = * = * = * =
* pCnclHdlr - Cancel handler. This routine checks the contents of
*             a 1-byte data are called Action. If it does not
*             contain a value of 'Q' (for quit) it resubmits
*             itself to batch, thus making it difficult to
*             cancel this particular program.
P pCnclHdlr       B                    Export

D pCnclHdlr       PI
D  OptionalPtr                    *    Options( *Omit )
D                                      Const
* Local data definitions
D SbmJob          C                    'SbmJob Job( NEP1 ) +
D                                      Cmd( Call NEP1 )'
```

continued

FIGURE 7.5 *CONTINUED*

```
D Action           S            1     Based( OptionalPtr )            Ⓐ

D As400Cmd         PR                 ExtPgm( 'QCMDEXC' )
D  Cmd                      500       Const
D  LenCmd                  15P 5 Const

 * If the Action data area is not 'Q' (for quit) then             Ⓑ
 * resubmit this job
C                  If           Action <> 'Q'
C                               And Action <> 'q'
C                  CallP        As400Cmd( SbmJob: %Size( SbmJob ) )
C                  EndIf

P pCnclHdlr        E
```

To facilitate passing the Action data area, I did a few things differently in NEP1 and NEP2 than in the NEP program. At **B** in Figure 7.4, the NEP1 module defines the ActionDtaAra as a 1-byte field that contains the contents of the Action data area. This definition is the same as the one in NEP. However, the next source line below it is unique to NEP1; it defines a pointer field called ActionPtr that's initialized to contain the address of the ActionDtaAra field. This definition is necessary because NEP1 must pass this pointer when registering pCnclHdlr as the cancel handler.

Another difference occurs at **A** in Figure 7.4, where the DlyJob (Delay Job) command appears. Notice, the delay time specified is 10 seconds. In the NEP program, the time specified was 60 seconds.

To see why I reduced the delay time so drastically, look at the main loop at **D**. I retrieve the contents of the data area upon each iteration through the loop. In the NEP program, I performed this retrieval once in the pCnclHdlr procedure. Because I wanted to show passing a value via a communication area, I transferred this data area retrieval up to the NEP1 program. The delay is only 10 seconds (instead of 60) because I didn't want to wait too long after changing the data area before testing the effects of canceling the program.

At **C,** I register pCnclHdlr as the cancel handler for the NEP1 program. The only difference between this and the NEP program is that a pointer to the communication area (ActionPtr) is passed as the second parameter (whereas *Omit was passed for this parameter in NEP). This pointer will be passed by the system to the pCnclHdlr procedure when the program is canceled.

Now let's move to program NEP2 in Figure 7.5. The control specification (or H-spec) at the start of this module identifies it as a module without a main procedure. In fact, this module contains only the subprocedure pCnclHdlr. This procedure is almost identical to its counterpart in program NEP, but there are some differences.

At **A,** a based 1-byte field called Action is defined. The basing pointer is actually the parameter passed to this procedure. As we discussed earlier, this parameter contains the address of the communication area. Therefore, the field called Action contains the contents of the Action data area. The If statement that inspects this data area (at **B**) differs from its counterpart in the NEP program because it uses this based Action field instead of directly accessing the ActionDtaAra field.

Summary

Although condition handlers are excellent for handling errors, they're powerless against unplanned cancellation of the job. In such cases, ILE cancel handlers can be quite handy. Cancel handlers receive control when a job is canceled for any reason. But protection against accidental cancellation isn't the only reason to use cancel handlers. Any time you need to clean up when a program is canceled is a good time to register a cancel handler.

Chapter 8

Invoking C Functions from an ILE RPG Program

ILE provides a rich mixed-language environment. This means it's easy to invoke user-written programs in other languages. In fact, from an ILE RPG program, you can invoke any C function documented in the C/C++ Run Time Library.

How are C functions mapped into an ILE environment? Actually, a C function is implemented as an ILE procedure, so you can prototype it in an ILE RPG program and then invoke it as if it were a regular ILE RPG subprocedure. This is precisely what we'll do in this chapter.

The C functions documented in the C/C++ Run Time Library are included in several service programs. Fortunately, you don't need to know the service programs' names because IBM provides a binding directory (called QC2LE) that names them. To gain access to the C/C++ Run Time Library, you need only include in your program a control specification that looks like this:

```
H BndDir( 'QC2LE' )
```

Interpreting C Documentation

To use C functions effectively, a typical ILE RPG programmer must develop the ability to interpret C reference documentation. The documentation to which I'll refer in this chapter is IBM's *C Library Reference* (SC09-2119). Let's start with a simple example from this manual.

Figure 8.1 shows an excerpt of the documentation for the C `log` function. A short description of the function appears at **A**. For our purposes, it isn't important that you understand the mathematical concept of a natural logarithm. My intent here is simply to explain how to interpret IBM's documentation.

At **B** is the name of the source physical file member that must be included in this source at compile time. This information pertains only to programs written in the C language and therefore has no direct bearing when you want to invoke C functions from an ILE RPG program. However, as you'll see, this information can come in handy at times.

The declaration at **C** is the prototype for the function:

```
double log(double x);
```

A C prototype serves the same purpose as an ILE RPG prototype. It tells the C compiler what value (if any) is returned by the function and what parameters (if any) must be passed to the function.

FIGURE 8.1

IBM Documentation for the C log *Function*

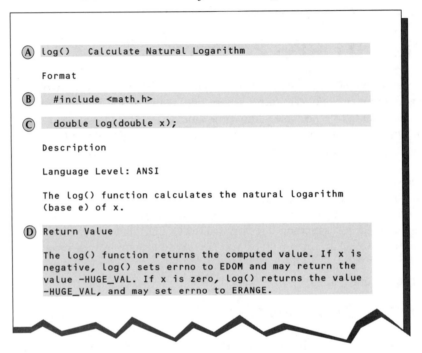

The first thing a C prototype tells you is what data type the function returns. The prototype at **C** indicates that the log function returns a field (or an *object*, as fields are called in C) of type double. A C type of double corresponds to an RPG double-precision floating-point field. Figure 8.2 shows the translation between some basic C data types and their ILE RPG counterparts.

If a C function returns no value, the specification would begin with the word *void*, as follows:

```
void assert(int expression);
```

The next portion of the prototype is simply the name (log) of the function. This name is followed by a parenthesized list of required parameters separated by commas. In the case of the prototype at **C**, there is a single parameter defined as **double x**. The word **double** indicates that this parameter must be a double-precision floating-point value. The name **x** is merely a formal name, very much the same as parameter names are in RPG prototypes. In other words, the parameter passed to this function doesn't need to be named **x**. It must, however, be a double-precision floating-point value.

FIGURE 8.2

Some C Data Types with Their RPG IV Counterparts

C type	RPG type or digits	Characters	Decimals
char	A	1	n/a
char *	*[1]	16[2]	n/a
float	F	4	n/a[3]
double	F	8	n/a[3]
long double	F	8	n/a[3]
short int[4]	I	5	0
unsigned short int[4]	U	5	0
int	I	10	0
long int[4]	I	10	0
unsigned int[4]	U	10	0
*[5]	*	n/a	n/a

[1] In C, a string is actually a pointer to a character string that is terminated with a null or X'00'.

[2] Pointers are 16 bytes long. In RPG, we don't specify a length for a pointer.

[3] You don't specify a number of decimals positions for a floating-point number because it can vary depending on the exponent portion of the number.

[4] You can abbreviate the types for short int, unsigned short int, long int, and unsigned int by dropping the int designation. For example, "unsigned" is an acceptable abbreviation for unsigned int.

[5] A type of * is a pointer type. In C, a pointer type is never coded merely as *. Instead it is preceded by a definite type, such as **int** * (pointer to an int) or **double** * (pointer to a double). C allows for an untyped pointer that is coded as **void** * (pointer to any C type). A pointer of type **void** * may point to any type of C object. Although one never specifies a length for a pointer, pointers are implemented as 16-byte fields on the AS/400.

Just as C functions don't have to return a value, they also don't have to require any parameters. If a C function requires no parameters, the list of parameters in the C prototype will consist of the single word **void**, as follows:

```
clock_t clock(void);
```

Let's summarize the prototype information for the **log** function. The function accepts a double-precision floating-point parameter and returns a double-precision floating-point value. Before an ILE RPG program can use this function, it must code an ILE RPG prototype that is equivalent to this C prototype. Here's how to do that:

```
D Log              PR              8F    ExtProc( 'log' )
D  InpVal                          8F    Value
```

Note that both the return value and the parameter are defined as 8F fields. That's because the C prototype specifies that they're both double fields and, as Figure 8.2 shows, 8F is the correct type to use for double fields in ILE RPG. The PR entry specifies the keyword ExtProc('log'). This says that the actual name of this procedure is 'log'. In general, ILE procedure names are case sensitive, so the name 'log' is different from the name 'Log'. This D-spec's name field, which indicates how I want to refer to the procedure in this ILE

RPG program, contains the value Log. D-spec names are case insensitive. So, in the program, I can refer to the C 'log' function as Log, LOG, or loG.

The D-spec following the PR line defines the single parameter required by the `log` function. In addition to specifying that the parameter is a double-precision floating-point field, this D-spec uses the Value keyword to specify that the parameter is passed by value. All C functions expect to receive parameters passed by value. Therefore, *you should always use the Value keyword for all parameters when prototyping a C function.*

Returning to the `log` function documentation in Figure 8.1, we see a more detailed description of the returned value at **D**. The natural logarithm math function can accept only positive numbers. This description tells you what happens if the function attempts to compute the natural logarithm of zero or a negative number. It says if the value is negative, C will set `errno` to EDOM. What does this mean?

The `errno` function is a standard way of communicating whether a C function succeeds. Because `errno` is a C function, it can be prototyped and invoked from an ILE RPG program like any other C function. I'll provide the details of how you gain access to this function in an ILE RPG program later in this chapter. For now, you need only understand that the `errno` function gives you access to an integer (RPG type I) field that contains a numeric code describing the error. If this `errno` value is 0, the C function didn't encounter an error.

EDOM is a C numeric constant that indicates a domain error. A C program gains access to the `errno` function and all the possible return values by specifying the following preprocessor directive:

```
#include <errno.h>
```

This is quite analogous to ILE RPG's /Copy precompiler directive. Unfortunately, ILE RPG programs don't have access to any similar set of /Copy modules. So a little extra research is necessary. This extra research is possible only if you have the C program product installed on your AS/400. The C runtime library is available on all AS/400 systems, but IBM-provided C source is available only with the C program product.

Whenever a C `#include` preprocessor directive specifies `<anything.h>`, it searches source physical files QSYSINC/H and QCLE/H for member ANYTHING. In this case, the `#include` will find member ERRNO in QCLE/H. Figure 8.3 shows the translations for the numeric constants defined in this member. C programmers can use these constants much as ILE RPG programmers use named constants. Therefore, as you can see from the first entry in Figure 8.3, when a C program specifies EDOM, it's actually referring to the numeric value 3001. An ILE RPG program can create a named constant EDOM as follows:

```
D EDOM            C                   3001
```

FIGURE 8.3
Translations for Numeric Constants Defined in <errno.h>

Constant	Numeric value	Description
EDOM	3001	Domain error in math function
ERANGE	3002	Range error in math function
ETRUNC	3003	Truncation on I/O operation
ENOTOPEN	3004	File has not been opened
ENOTREAD	3005	File not opened for read
ERECIO	3008	File opened for record I/O
ENOTWRITE	3009	File not opened for write
ESTDIN	3010	`stdin` cannot be opened
ESTDOUT	3011	`stdout` cannot be opened
ESTDERR	3012	`stderr` cannot be opened
EBADSEEK	3013	Bad offset to seek to
EBADNAME	3014	Invalid file name specified
EBADMODE	3015	Invalid file mode specified
EBADPOS	3017	Invalid position specifier
ENOPOS	3018	No record at specified position
ENUMMBRS	3019	No `ftell` if more than one member
ENUMRECS	3020	No `ftell` if too many records
EBADFUNC	3022	Invalid function pointer
ENOREC	3026	Record not found
EBADDATA	3028	Message data invalid
EBADOPT	3040	Bad option on I/O function
ENOTUPD	3041	File not opened for update
ENOTDLT	3042	File not opened for delete
EPAD	3043	Padding occurred on write operation
EBADKEYLN	3044	Bad key length option
EPUTANDGET	3080	Illegal write after read
EGETANDPUT	3081	Illegal read after write
EIOERROR	3101	I/O exception nonrecoverable error
EIORECERR	3102	I/O exception recoverable error
EINVAL	3021	Invalid argument
EIO	3006	I/O error
ENODEV	3007	No such device
EBUSY	3029	Resource busy
ENOENT	3025	No such file or library
EPERM	3027	Operation not permitted

The log function documentation at **D** in Figure 8.1 refers to another constant —
HUGE_VAL — which is supposed to represent infinity in a floating-point field. Through
experimentation, I've found that HUGE_VAL is actually the hexadecimal value
X'7FF0000000000000' stored in a double-precision floating-point field. –HUGE_VAL is
X'FFF0000000000000'. An ILE RPG program can create a field called HUGE_VAL as follows.

```
D                   DS
D Char8                            8    Inz( X'7FF0000000000000' )
D HUGE_VAL                         8F   Overlay( Char8 )
```

An ILE RPG program can refer to HUGE_VAL or –HUGE_VAL using this definition.

A Sample Program Using the C log Function

Figure 8.4 shows ILE RPG program Log, which uses the C log function.

FIGURE 8.4

ILE RPG Program Log

```
Ⓐ  H BndDir( 'QC2LE' )

Ⓑ  D Log              PR          8F   ExtProc( 'log' )
   D   InpVal                     8F   Value

Ⓒ  D GetErr           PR          *    ExtProc( '__errno' )
   D   DummyPrm                   1    Options( *Omit )

   D NumFloat8        S           8F
   D LogVal           S           8F
   D DummyVar         S           1
Ⓓ  D ErrNo            S          10I 0 Based( ErrNoPtr )

   * Negative return values
   D EDOM             C           3001
   D ERANGE           C           3002

   D                  DS
   D Char8                        8    Inz( X'7FF0000000000000' )
   D HUGE_VAL                     8F   Overlay( Char8 )

Ⓔ  D PrmNum           S          15P 5

   C      *Entry      Plist
   C                  Parm                      PrmNum

Ⓕ  * Convert the parameter to double-precision floating-point
   C                  Eval        NumFloat8 = PrmNum

   * Invoke the C log function
   C                  Eval        LogVal = Log( NumFloat8 )
```

continued

FIGURE 8.4 *CONTINUED*

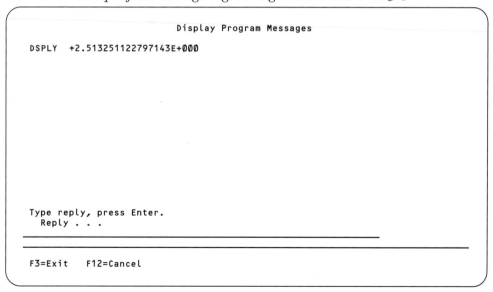

```
* Get the C errno return code
C                     Eval      ErrNoPtr = GetErr( *Omit )

* Test for errors
C                     If             ErrNo  = EDOM
C                     Or ErrNo  = ERANGE
C                     Or LogVal = HUGE_VAL
C                     Or LogVal = -HUGE_VAL
C        'log failed' Dsply                    DummyVar
C                     Else
C        LogVal       Dsply                    DummyVar
C                     EndIf

C                     Eval      *INLR = *On
```

The program accepts a single numeric parameter, calculates the natural logarithm, and displays the result. Here's an example of how to invoke this program from the AS/400 command line:

`Call Log 1.2345`

Figure 8.5 shows the result of calling this program with the 1.2345 parameter.

FIGURE 8.5

Output from Calling Program Log with Parameter 1.2345

```
                        Display Program Messages

   DSPLY   +2.513251122797143E+000

















   Type reply, press Enter.
      Reply . . .



   F3=Exit    F12=Cancel
```

The value shown (+2.513251122797143E+000) is an ILE RPG float literal. The value following the letter E (+000) is the exponent of 10 to multiply by the value to its left (+2.513251122797143). So this literal represents the value $2.513251122797143 \times 10^0$.

Because $10^0 = 1$, the value displayed in Figure 8.5 is actually 2.513251122797143. This is the approximate natural logarithm of 1.2345. It's approximate (but close enough for most applications) because the actual value cannot be expressed with a finite set of decimal digits.

Notice at **A** in Figure 8.4 that I've specified the binding directory QC2LE in the control specification. As I mentioned earlier, you should always use this control specification when you want to access any C library function. The prototype for the C log function appears at **B**.

At **C**, I've coded the prototype for the C errno function. The errno function's real name is __errno (two underscore characters preceding the errno name). In the RPG program, I refer to this function as GetErr, as shown in the PR statement at **C**. Notice, this function returns a pointer. I've also specified a dummy parameter with Options(*Omit). As I explained in Chapter 3, this technique lets me invoke procedures that don't require any parameters in such a way that it's clear that the referenced name is a procedure rather than a data name.

Earlier, I stated that errno gives you access to a C int type field (an ILE RPG-type integer with 10 digits and zero decimals). In reality, errno returns a pointer to a C int object. At **D**, I define the based integer (ErrNo) that will be used for this purpose. At **G**, I invoke the errno function by specifying GetErr(*Omit) and placing the function's return value into the field ErrNoPtr. Notice at **D**, ErrNoPtr is the basing pointer for the field ErrNo. Therefore, the Eval statement at **G** is giving the ILE RPG program access to the C errno value. After this Eval statement is executed, the program can refer to this value by referencing the ErrNo based field.

The *Entry Plist statement at **E** indicates that this program accepts a packed 15,5 field as its sole parameter. I defined this parameter as a packed 15,5 field so it can be passed more easily from the command line. But it must be converted to a double-precision floating-point field to be passed to the C log function. The first Eval statement at **F** does this. The next Eval statement at **F** invokes the C log function. (Actually, I could have passed PrmNum as a parameter to the log function even though it's not a double-precision floating-point number. Because the parameter is passed by value, the system will convert it to the proper format for me. However, I felt the code would be clearer if I did the conversion explicitly as shown.)

After the program invokes the log function, the Eval statement at **G** gives the program access to the C errno value. The If statement following this Eval statement checks for the possible error conditions described at **D** in Figure 8.1. If the program detects an error, it displays the message 'log failed'. Otherwise, it displays the value (LogVal) returned by the log function.

Now let's look at a more complicated C library function.

The C bsearch Library Function

The C library bsearch function performs a binary search on an array. A binary search is an array lookup that can be far faster than the normal serial search.

A binary search can be done only when the array is arranged in ascending or descending sequence. However, the `bsearch` function requires the array to be in ascending sequence.

To understand how a binary search works, imagine you want to look up a word in a dictionary. Would you perform a *serial search*? That is, would you start with the first word in the dictionary and read forward until you found the word you're looking for? Of course not! But the RPG LookUp command always performs a serial search — even if the array is arranged in order.

When you're searching for a word, you'd typically guess where the word is in the dictionary and go there directly. When you examine the page you've chosen, there are three possibilities:

1. You guessed right.
2. The word is before the current page.
3. The word is after the current page.

Even if the word you're looking for is before or after the current page, you've quickly eliminated perhaps several hundred pages of the dictionary from consideration. And you can repeat this step to quickly find the page you're looking for. Because each step of this process can eliminate many hundreds of pages of words from consideration, this approach is much more efficient than a straight serial search, which would eliminate only one word at a time.

A binary search works much the same as our dictionary example. It examines an array element that is located roughly halfway through the set of elements in the array. The binary search then determines whether this array element is the element it's looking for or is before or after the element it's looking for. If the sought-after array element is before the current element, the binary search examines the element that's roughly halfway between the beginning of the array and the current element. If the sought-after element is after the current element, the binary search examines an array element that's roughly halfway between the current element and the end of the array. The search continues narrowing down the array elements examined until it either finds what it's looking for or determines that the sought-after element doesn't exist in the array.

Of course, a serial search will be faster if the element you're looking for happens to be near the beginning of the array. But if the search arguments are random values, a serial search will, on average, turn up the correct element after searching roughly half the array elements. A binary search for a larger array will be much faster than that. For example, suppose you have an array that contains 2,000 elements sorted in ascending sequence. On average, a serial search can find a designated element after examining about 1,000 elements. A binary search will find the element after examining a maximum of 10 array elements.

Naturally, this dramatic improvement becomes less pronounced as the number of array elements shrinks. If your array has only 10 elements, it probably doesn't matter how you search it. Also, a binary search must perform more work than a serial search to determine which element to examine next. A serial search simply adds 1 to the index of the previous element examined. But a binary search determines the next element number to examine by dividing the number of candidate elements by 2 and adding or subtracting this value to or from the current candidate element (adding if the candidate element is less than the looked-for value, and subtracting otherwise). The serial search needs to keep track of only the array element currently being examined. A binary search must keep track of the current element being examined as well as the lower and upper indexes of the current range of candidate array elements. For these reasons, I believe it doesn't benefit you much to use a binary search for less than 50 array elements.

Unfortunately, ILE RPG has no binary search instruction. Although you can code your own binary search in ILE RPG, it's easier (and safer!) to use the C library `bsearch` function. Figure 8.6 shows the IBM documentation for this function.

As you can see, the `bsearch` function is far more complicated than the `log` function. But if you understand this discussion and the subsequent example using the `bsearch` function, you'll be well on your way to fully understanding how to use C library functions in an ILE RPG program. Seatbelt fastened? Let's get started!

The `#include` and C prototype for the `bsearch` function appear at **A** in Figure 8.6. Although an ILE RPG program cannot /Copy (the ILE RPG equivalent of C's `#include`) any members that include the ILE RPG equivalent of the `<stdlib.h>` source member, it's nonetheless useful to know that member STDLIB in source physical file QCLE/H contains some critical information useful to C programs. We'll see why this is true in a moment.

The prototype starts out with `void *bsearch`. Remember that a function that returns `void` doesn't return a value. Despite including `void`, however, this function actually returns a pointer. The `*` character that butts against the name of the function (`bsearch`) is actually part of what's being returned by the function. In other words, the `bsearch` function returns `void *`, which is a pointer to any type of C object. A somewhat circuitous description of this return value appears at **E** in Figure 8.6. This documentation states that the return value is a pointer to the array element that is being sought. It further states that if the sought-after array element isn't found, the returned pointer will be NULL.

The prototype at **A** defines five parameters that must be passed to the `bsearch` function. The first parameter is defined as

```
const void *key
```

The description of this parameter starts out with the keyword `const`. I'll describe what `const` means shortly. The actual type for this parameter is `void *`. This means it's a pointer to a C object of any type.

The `const` keyword that precedes the `void *` specification is useful for parameters that are pointers. Recall that C parameters are always passed by value. This means that a function can safely modify a parameter without modifying the original object. However, whenever a pointer is being passed, the invoked function may be able to use the pointer to gain access to the C object to which the pointer points. The function could then modify that object. The `const` keyword is a promise (that's not 100 percent software-enforceable) that the function won't modify the object to which the parameter points. At **C** in Figure 8.6, we see that this parameter (whose formal name is `key`) is the value being looked for in the array.

FIGURE 8.6

IBM Documentation for the C bsearch *Function*

```
bsearch() -- Search Arrays

Format

    #include <stdlib.h>
    void *bsearch(const void *key, const void *base,
                  size_t num, size_t size,
                  int (*compare)(const void *key, const void *element));
```
(A)

Description

Language Level: ANSI

The bsearch() function performs a binary search of an array of num elements, each of size bytes. The array must be sorted in ascending order by the function pointed to by compare.   (B)

The base is a pointer to the base of the array to search, and key is the value being sought.   (C)

The compare argument is a pointer to a function you must supply that compares two items and returns a value specifying their relationship. The first item in the argument list of the compare() function is the pointer to the value of the item that is being searched for.   (D)

The second item in the argument list of the compare() function is a pointer to the array element being compared with the key. The compare() function must compare the key value with the array element and then return one of the following values:

```
Value                 Meaning

Less than 0           key less than element

0                     key identical to element

Greater than 0        key greater than element
```

Return Value

The bsearch() function returns a pointer to key in the array to which base points.   (E)
If two keys are equal, the element that key will point to is unspecified. If the bsearch() function cannot find the key, it returns NULL.

The `bsearch` function's second parameter (`base`) is a pointer as well. Once again, the `const` keyword assures us that the `bsearch` function won't modify the object being pointed to. The description at **C** tells us that this is a pointer to the beginning of the array.

The third parameter (`num`) has a type of `size_t`. A quick look at the basic types in Figure 8.2 tells you that `size_t` isn't one of them. So what is `size_t`? Recall from **A** in Figure 8.6 that a C programmer must code `#include <stdlib.h>` to use the `bsearch` function. This `#include` member corresponds to member STDLIB in source physical file QCLE/H. This member contains (in part) the following lines of code:

```
#ifndef   __size_t
  #define __size_t
  typedef unsigned int size_t
#endif
```

The `typedef` directive defines `size_t` as unsigned int. This means that whenever you code `size_t` in a C program that has specified `#include <stdlib.h>`, you're actually specifying unsigned int. Figure 8.2 shows that this type corresponds to an ILE RPG type of U with 10 digits and zero decimal positions. So although an RPG programmer can't make direct use of the `#include` members that a C programmer must use, at times it's helpful to examine these members to gain necessary information. The description at **B** in Figure 8.6 makes it clear that this parameter (whose formal name is `num`) is the number of array elements. Note also at **B** that the array must be arranged in ascending sequence.

The fourth parameter (`size`) is also defined to have type `size_t` (and therefore unsigned int). The description at **B** in Figure 8.6 tells us that this parameter is the size in bytes of each array element.

The fifth element specified in the prototype at **A** is a bit complicated. First, its type is int. Again, Figure 8.2 tells us this is an ILE RPG type of I with 10 digits and zero decimal positions. The formal name of this parameter is (`*compare`). Whenever a name is specified as (`*anything`), it's actually a pointer to a function. In our case, the formal name (not the actual name) of the function is `compare`. This parameter is really a pointer to a function that returns an int (or ILE RPG 10I 0) type. This function is expected to be provided (i.e., written) by the user of the `bsearch` function, so the parameter is actually a pointer to a user-written procedure. In ILE RPG, a pointer to a procedure must be identified with the ProcPtr (procedure pointer) keyword. We'll see how this works in the upcoming example.

Because this parameter points to a function (or ILE procedure), the prototype must tell us what value the function returns and what parameters the function requires. The `int` preceding the formal function name tells us that this function returns an int value. Once again, Figure 8.2 tells us that this C type is equivalent to an RPG type of I with 10 digits and zero decimal positions. The parameters that are passed to this user-written procedure are defined following the formal name of (`*compare`). They are defined as follows:

```
(const void *key, const void *element)
```

The `compare` function requires two parameters. The first parameter (`key`) is a C type of `void *` and is therefore a pointer to an object of any type. The description at **D** in

Figure 8.6 tells us that this parameter is a pointer to the key value (i.e., the sought-after value).

The second parameter (`element`) required by the compare function is also a pointer to an object of any type. The description at **D** tells us that this is a pointer to an array element.

The last part of the description at **D** explains the action this function must perform and the value that must be returned. It tells us that the function must compare the key value to the array element and set the return value depending on the outcome of this comparison. It must set the return value to 0 if the key value is equal to the array element. It must set the return value to a negative number if the key value is less than the array element. Finally, it must set the return value to a positive number if the key value is larger than the array element.

Note the versatility of the `bsearch` function. Because the `compare` function is user-written, `bsearch` itself doesn't require knowledge of the format of the array elements. The only software that needs this knowledge during the running of the `bsearch` function is the user-written `compare` function. This lets `bsearch` perform a binary search on arrays where the elements are of any type. The `compare` function can even make up its own collating sequence. For example, it could make case-insensitive compare operations, and the `bsearch` function would work just fine as long as the array is arranged in ascending, case-insensitive order.

Now let's consider an example that actually uses the `bsearch` function.

The BSearch Program

The ILE RPG BSearch program uses the C `bsearch` function to search a compile-time array containing the following city names: Albuquerque, Boston, Chicago, Denver, Fairbanks, Honolulu, Indianapolis, Los Angeles, New York, and Omaha.

The program accepts a (case-sensitive) city name as its sole parameter. It then uses the C `bsearch` function to determine whether the parameter passed matches one of the array entries. For example, if you invoke this program with the following AS/400 command

```
Call BSearch Parm( 'Chicago' )
```

the program will display the screen shown in Figure 8.7. The message simply states that the entry 'Chicago' was found in the array. If you call the program passing a city name that's not in the array, the program displays the 'Not Found' message.

FIGURE 8.7

Output After Invoking the BSearch Program with Parameter = 'Chicago'

```
                          Display Program Messages

 DSPLY   Found




 Type reply, press Enter.
   Reply . . .
 _____


 F3=Exit    F12=Cancel
```

Figure 8.8 shows the source for the BSearch program.

FIGURE 8.8

ILE RPG Program BSearch

```
     H BndDir( 'QC2LE' )

(A)  D FindIt          PR                  *    ExtProc( 'bsearch' )
     D  LookFor                            *    Value
     D  DataStart                          *    Value
     D  Elements                        10U 0 Value
     D  Size                            10U 0 Value
     D  CompFunc                           *    ProcPtr Value

(B)  D CompCity        PR              10I 0
     D  LookFor                            *    Value
     D  ArrElt                             *    Value

     D EltSize         S              15    Based( DummyPtr )

     D CityLkup        S                    Like( EltSize )
(C)  D CityArr         S                    Like( EltSize )
     D                                      Dim( 10 )
     D                                      CtData
     D DummyVar        S               1

     D FndElt          S                    Like( EltSize )
     D                                      Based( FndEltPtr )
```

continued

FIGURE 8.8 *CONTINUED*

```
C           *Entry        Plist                                                D
C                         Parm                      CityLkup

C                         Eval        FndEltPtr =
C                                         FindIt( %Addr( CityLkup ):
C                                         %Addr( CityArr ):
C                                         %Elem( CityArr ):
C                                         %Size( CityArr ):
C                                         %Paddr( 'COMPCITY' ) )

C                         If          FndEltPtr = *Null
C           'Not Found'   Dsply                     DummyVar
C                         Else
C           'Found'       Dsply                     DummyVar
C                         EndIf

C                         Eval        *INLR = *On
```

```
P CompCity      B                                                             E
D CompCity      PI            10I 0
D  LookFor                       *    Value
D  ArrEltPtr                     *    Value

D Key           S                    Like( EltSize )                          F
D                                    Based( LookFor )
D ArrElt        S                    Like( EltSize )
D                                    Based( ArrEltPtr )
D RetVal        S            10I 0

C                         Select

C                         When        Key < ArrElt
C                         Eval        RetVal = -1

C                         When        Key = ArrElt
C                         Eval        RetVal = 0

C                         When        Key > ArrElt
C                         Eval        RetVal = +1

C                         EndSl

C                         Return      RetVal

P CompCity      E
```

```
**                                                                            G
Albuquerque
Boston
Chicago
Denver
Fairbanks
Honolulu
Indianapolis
Los Angeles
New York
Omaha
```

The ILE RPG prototype for the C bsearch function appears at **A**. The first source line specifies that I'll refer to the bsearch function as FindIt in the program. Notice I specify that this function returns a pointer by coding * (for pointer) in the type field on the PR D-spec. This is in accordance with the fact that the C prototype (**A** in Figure 8.6) indicates that the bsearch function returns a pointer. The five parameters I described earlier are then defined in the next five lines of the prototype at **A**. Notice that the last parameter (CompFunc) is defined as a pointer type and uses the keyword ProcPtr. This makes it a procedure pointer. Recall, this parameter is a pointer to the compare function. In ILE RPG, a pointer to a function (or subprocedure, in this case) must be defined as a procedure pointer.

At **B** is the prototype for the compare function. In this case, I am calling this procedure CompCity. As we saw earlier, this procedure must accept two parameters: a pointer (LookFor) to the field containing the key value and a pointer (ArrElt) to the array element being compared to the key value. Note that this procedure is automatically invoked (potentially multiple times) by the bsearch function, not by the programmer. Remember, the compare function is used by bsearch to learn the outcome of a comparison that bsearch has decided to make.

The array being searched is called CityArr and is defined at **C**. The CtData keyword says this is a compile-time array. The compile-time data for the array appears at **G**.

The main routine is at **D**. The program accepts a single parameter called CityLkup, which is specified by the caller. This is the name of the city that you want looked up in array CityArr. The Eval statement is really invoking the bsearch function. Because all parameters are being passed by value, they can be expressions. This lets me specify all five parameters as the return value of ILE RPG built-in functions.

Recall that the IBM documentation states that the returned value will be NULL if bsearch is unable to find the key value in the array. The If statement at **D** following the Eval statement tests this condition. If the returned value is NULL (or *Null in ILE RPG), the program displays the 'Not Found' message. Otherwise, it displays the 'Found' message.

Now let's look at the compare function, which is called CompCity and implemented at **E**. The first parameter (LookFor) is a pointer to the key value. Notice at **F**, I define a based standalone field called Key, where the basing pointer is this first parameter. Similarly, because the second parameter is a pointer to the array element being compared, I've defined (at **F**) a based field called ArrElt, whose basing pointer is the second parameter. Therefore, in this subprocedure, whenever I refer to Key, I'm actually referring to the key value whose address was passed as the first parameter to this subprocedure. Similarly, a reference in this subprocedure to ArrElt is actually a reference to the array element whose address was passed as the second parameter to this procedure.

Recall that this procedure must compare the two elements and return an integer data type whose value is negative, 0, or positive depending on the outcome of the comparison. I've chosen –1 and +1 as my negative and positive return values. The Select/EndSl block implements this logic. It sets the field RetVal to –1 when the key field is less than the array element. It sets RetVal to 0 when the key field is equal to the array element.

Finally, it sets RetVal to +1 when the key field is larger than the array element. This sets RetVal in accordance with the IBM documentation at **D** in Figure 8.6.

The subprocedure ends by returning the value to the **bsearch** function that invoked it.

Summary

ILE RPG lets you prototype and use any of the C library functions. In effect, this extends the RPG language to include many standard functions provided in C. The main skill that most ILE RPG programmers must develop to use C functions in an ILE RPG program is the ability to read and understand the IBM documentation for these functions.

Appendix A

ILE Optimization

On the AS/400, *optimization* means maximizing the runtime performance of a program or service program. At run time, highly optimized programs or service programs should run faster than their non-optimized equivalents.

You can specify an optimization level for any ILE program or service program at compile time. The software that performs this task is called the *optimizing translator*. You can also change the optimization level at any time after a program or service program has been created, by using the ChgPgm (Change Program) or ChgSrvPgm (Change Service Program) command. Be aware that using ChgPgm or ChgSrvPgm to change the optimization level removes the listing view from a program that has been compiled with DbgView(*List).

ILE defines four optimization levels:

- 10 or *None
- 20 or *Basic
- 30 or *Full
- 40 (more than optimization level 30 — not available in ILE RPG)

In general, the higher the optimization level, the faster the program should run. However, with improved performance, you pay a price with reduced debugging and problem-determination capability. When the optimization level is 20 or higher, you can't rely on the debugger to display the current value of a variable. The optimizing translator places some variables into registers. But because the debugger is unaware of which fields have been optimized into registers, you can't assume the value displayed by the debugger is the actual value of the variable.

For this reason, IBM recommends that you don't optimize when testing your programs. After testing a program, you may (or may not) elect to use the ChgPgm command or recompile the program and specify a higher optimization level.

Another thing the ILE optimizing translator can do is rearrange instructions. When it does this, the system may not be able to figure out the exact line number that causes a program exception. If this happens, the system will display multiple possible line numbers. Obviously, this behavior can make problem determination a bit tougher. You should consider this eventuality before deciding whether you want to use the ILE optimizer.

Appendix B

Sample Programs: SNTP Client and Server

The following description of Internet time protocols originally appeared in the article "Visual Basic Sockets Program Sets PC Clock" (NEWS/400, March 1999) by Terry Smith. It is excerpted with permission.

Internet Time Protocols

Internet Request for Comment (RFC) 1305 describes a mechanism called Network Time Protocol (NTP) for synchronizing computer clocks across the Internet to within a few hundred picoseconds of accuracy. This kind of accuracy requires complex algorithms and synchronization with multiple sources. RFC 2030 describes a simpler method for synchronizing network clocks called Simple Network Time Protocol (SNTP). SNTP describes a specification that uses the same transmission format as NTP but doesn't require the same processing overhead and computation complexities. SNTP synchronization is accurate to within a few milliseconds, which is more than adequate for most applications.

Your CD contains software for ILE RPG programs SNTPCLNT and SNTPSRVR, which are SNTP client and server programs, respectively. You can use SNTPCLNT to synchronize with any SNTP or NTP server. For example, you could use SNTPCLNT to synchronize your AS/400's clock with the U.S. Naval NTP server at URL *tick.usno.navy.mil* on the Internet. You could also synchronize with another AS/400 running an SNTP or NTP server. The SNTPSRVR program will suffice for this purpose.

The basis for time synchronization described by RFCs 1305 and 2030 is the NTP message format, which consists of a number of bits and bytes used for control and reference information and a series of timestamp fields for time information. Each timestamp field consists of a 64-bit number. The first 32 bits represent the number of seconds since midnight (0 hour, or 0h) on 1 January 1900. The second 32 bits store the fraction of a second. For consistency, all timestamps are stored as Greenwich Mean Time (GMT). Figure B.1 shows the NTP message format and timestamp format.

Figure B.1
NTP Message Format and Timestamp Format

NTP message format

```
                    1                   2                   3
0 1 2 3 4 5 6 7 8 9 0 1 2 3 4 5 6 7 8 9 0 1 2 3 4 5 6 7 8 9 0 1
+-+-+-+-+-+-+-+-+-+-+-+-+-+-+-+-+-+-+-+-+-+-+-+-+-+-+-+-+-+-+-+-+
|LI | VN |Mode |    Stratum    |     Poll      |   Precision   |
+-+-+-+-+-+-+-+-+-+-+-+-+-+-+-+-+-+-+-+-+-+-+-+-+-+-+-+-+-+-+-+-+
|                         Root delay                           |
+-+-+-+-+-+-+-+-+-+-+-+-+-+-+-+-+-+-+-+-+-+-+-+-+-+-+-+-+-+-+-+-+
|                       Root dispersion                        |
+-+-+-+-+-+-+-+-+-+-+-+-+-+-+-+-+-+-+-+-+-+-+-+-+-+-+-+-+-+-+-+-+
|                     Reference identifier                     |
+-+-+-+-+-+-+-+-+-+-+-+-+-+-+-+-+-+-+-+-+-+-+-+-+-+-+-+-+-+-+-+-+
|                                                              |
|                  Reference timestamp (64)                    |
|                                                              |
+-+-+-+-+-+-+-+-+-+-+-+-+-+-+-+-+-+-+-+-+-+-+-+-+-+-+-+-+-+-+-+-+
|                                                              |
|                  Originate timestamp (64)                    |
|                                                              |
+-+-+-+-+-+-+-+-+-+-+-+-+-+-+-+-+-+-+-+-+-+-+-+-+-+-+-+-+-+-+-+-+
|                                                              |
|                   Receive timestamp (64)                     |
|                                                              |
+-+-+-+-+-+-+-+-+-+-+-+-+-+-+-+-+-+-+-+-+-+-+-+-+-+-+-+-+-+-+-+-+
|                                                              |
|                  Transmit timestamp (64)                     |
|                                                              |
+-+-+-+-+-+-+-+-+-+-+-+-+-+-+-+-+-+-+-+-+-+-+-+-+-+-+-+-+-+-+-+-+
|                Key identifier (optional) (32)                |
+-+-+-+-+-+-+-+-+-+-+-+-+-+-+-+-+-+-+-+-+-+-+-+-+-+-+-+-+-+-+-+-+
|                                                              |
|                                                              |
|                Message digest (optional) (128)               |
|                                                              |
|                                                              |
+-+-+-+-+-+-+-+-+-+-+-+-+-+-+-+-+-+-+-+-+-+-+-+-+-+-+-+-+-+-+-+-+
```

NTP timestamp format

```
                    1                   2                   3
0 1 2 3 4 5 6 7 8 9 0 1 2 3 4 5 6 7 8 9 0 1 2 3 4 5 6 7 8 9 0 1
+-+-+-+-+-+-+-+-+-+-+-+-+-+-+-+-+-+-+-+-+-+-+-+-+-+-+-+-+-+-+-+-+
|                           Seconds                            |
+-+-+-+-+-+-+-+-+-+-+-+-+-+-+-+-+-+-+-+-+-+-+-+-+-+-+-+-+-+-+-+-+
|                  Seconds fraction (0-padded)                 |
+-+-+-+-+-+-+-+-+-+-+-+-+-+-+-+-+-+-+-+-+-+-+-+-+-+-+-+-+-+-+-+-+
```

To use the NTP message format to synchronize computer clocks, a client program first sets the Mode field in the message format to indicate that a request for time is being made (client mode). Optionally, the client places the current time of the client machine into the Transmit timestamp field, which can be used upon return of the message from the NTP server to compute the round-trip delay of the exchange.

After setting these fields, the client sends the message to an NTP server program using the sockets interface and the port reserved for NTP use, port 123. The NTP server program receives the message on port 123 and then initializes the fields in the NTP message as follows. First, the server sets the Receive timestamp field to the time that the request was received. Next, the Transmit timestamp value sent by the client is copied into the Originate timestamp field so it can be sent back to the client and used to compute the round-trip delay. The Mode field is set to indicate a server response, and some control fields in the first part of the message are set to identify the server's mode of operation. Finally, the server places the current time into the Transmit timestamp and sends the message back to the client.

Upon receipt of the message, the client computes the round-trip delay and the difference between the server clock's time and the client clock's time (this difference is called the *local clock offset*). Once this difference is computed, the client can decide whether to update the local clock.

Computers using this method of time synchronization are classified in different strata. Computers directly synchronized with an atomic clock source are in stratum 1. Computers synchronized with a level 1 or other NTP server using NTP or SNTP are in strata 2 through 15, depending on the level of the server with which they're synchronized.

There is much more involved in understanding exactly how to implement the SNTP protocol than I've presented here. You can read more about it on the Web at *http://www.uni-bayreuth.de/rfc/rfc2030.txt*.

Appendix C

Using a Blackboard Service Program

Adapted with permission from the article "Using Blackboards with Trigger Programs" by Mike Cravitz (NEWS/400, April 1999).

The CD that accompanies this book contains code that shows how an AS/400 trigger and its underlying application can communicate with each other.

Trigger programs sometimes need access to more information than is available in the trigger buffer. Don't get me wrong! The trigger buffer (automatically passed to the trigger program as the first of two parameters) has a lot of very useful information. But sometimes it's simply not enough. For instance, a trigger program might want to be instructed whether it should perform field editing or not. A trusted program might instruct the trigger to bypass editing in order to improve I/O performance.

I'll outline a technique you can use to communicate any information you might want between an application and a trigger. Here, I use the term *application* to mean the program that performed the database action resulting in the trigger being invoked. But before going further, let's have a quick overview of AS/400 triggers.

A trigger is a program written by the user (as opposed to IBM developers) that is automatically invoked (or "fired") by IBM database management when a database action such as adding, changing, or deleting a record occurs. By issuing the AddPfTrg (Add Physical File Trigger) command, you can define a trigger to be invoked in any combination of the following six situations: before insert, before update, before delete, after insert, after update, and after delete.

Database management passes two parameters to the trigger program: the trigger buffer and the trigger buffer length. The trigger buffer contains a lot of useful information, including the file name and library, which of the six possible events (e.g., before insert) caused the trigger to be fired, commitment control information, and the old and new record images.

Parts Is Parts

A client of mine (Big Company, or BC) recently acquired a smaller company (Little Company, or LC). After acquiring LC, BC noticed a lot of useful application software running on LC's AS/400s. Although BC didn't intend to use this software for its own operations, the company saw that the software was useful for running LC's business. So BC decided to continue using LC's software for LC. BC also decided to keep LC's inventory numbering system, even though it was incompatible with BC's. However, BC also had to assign BC-style item numbers to LC's inventory items so they could be tracked with BC's application software.

BC's proposed solution was a cross-reference file containing a keyed list of LC items, their LC item numbers, and their corresponding BC item numbers. Whenever LC added a new item to its inventory, a trigger would assign a corresponding BC item number and update the cross-reference file and BC's inventory file.

As we discussed this solution, we considered how to handle cases in which BC didn't want the trigger to perform its action. For example, LC ran promotions for which it automatically added a sample item to every order. For these sample items, LC assigned a temporary item number. BC didn't want the cross-reference file updated with temporary item numbers because BC's software didn't need to know those item numbers. I suggested that BC could use the RmvPfTrg (Remove Physical File Trigger) command to remove the trigger before running the application that inserts the temporary item numbers. However, BC worried that someone might easily forget to remove the trigger when doing this. So I told them of another solution: the blackboard technique.

The Blackboard Jungle

A *blackboard* is a service program with no executable code. It simply defines data using the Export keyword, thus making that exported data commonly available to any program within a job that binds to the blackboard. An application can place data into a blackboard, and when the trigger is invoked, it will see that data. The trigger also can place data into the blackboard, and when the trigger is completed, the application will see the data.

A blackboard uses service program data exports (procedures and data that are available to programs that use a service program) to export data only. All programs in a call stack that access a particular service program and run in the same activation group as the service program have access to the same exported data. An RPG program references exported data from a service program by defining it in a D-spec exactly as it's defined in the service program, except using the Import keyword. (The service program defines the same data, but it uses the Export keyword.)

Figure C.1 shows a blackboard service program with its data exports.

FIGURE C.1

Overview of Blackboard Service Program

Any program with procedures on the call stack that reference the blackboard service program has read and modify access to this data. In particular, if the application and the trigger programs both reference the blackboard service program, they can both read and modify the exported data.

The Sample Trigger

Let's return now to my client's inventory cross-reference problem. I mocked up a sample of the blackboard technique for BC. To produce a more complete example, I assumed the existence of a customer cross-reference file as well as an item cross-reference file. The trigger's job was to update both cross-reference files by way of the blackboard whenever the application told it to do so.

Figure C.2 shows the blackboard data specifications as they're defined in the blackboard service program (BoardSvc).

FIGURE C.2

Blackboard Data Specification in Service Program BoardSvc

```
D BlkBoard         DS                        Export
D   ApplPgmName              10              Inz( 'NoPgm' )
D   UpdCustFlg                  N            Inz( *On )
D   UpdItemFlg                  N            Inz( *On )
D   OtherData               100             Inz( *ALL' ' )
```

Although they aren't referenced in the trigger program sample code presented here, I show how you can define fields to hold the name of the application program as well as other data. The only two fields that are actually used are UpdCustFlg and UpdItemFlg. These are defined as indicator variables (type N), which means they assume one of two values: *On or *Off. If the application wants to suppress the update of the customer cross-reference file for a customer insert operation, it should ensure that UpdCustFlg has the value *Off before performing the insert. Similarly, if the application wants to suppress an update of the item cross-reference file, it should set UpdItemFlg to *Off before inserting a new item.

Figure C.3 shows the trigger program code that tests the appropriate flag.

FIGURE C.3

Trigger Code That Checks the Blackboard Flag Fields

```
        .
        .
        .
* Invoke the update routine in the event the application
* says it's okay to do so.
C                 If          UpdCustFlg  = *On
C                             And     TbFile = 'CUSTOMER'
C                 ExSr        UpdCustXref
C                 EndIf

C                 If          UpdItemFlg  = *On
C                             And     TbFile = 'ITEM'
C                 ExSr        UpdItemXref
C                 EndIf
        .
        .
        .
```

The field TbFile contains the name (from the trigger buffer) of the file that fired the trigger. If the file is the customer file and the application has given the go-ahead to update the cross-reference (i.e., if UpdCustFlg = *On), the trigger executes the UpdCustXref subroutine. A similar test is performed for the item file. I don't show these subroutines because they're simply supposed to perform the mundane task of assigning a corresponding BC number for the LC number and placing that entry into the cross-reference file. Because showing how to code this subroutine isn't the point of the example, my UpdCustXref and UpdItemXref subroutines simply write a record to the cross-reference file without filling in the values for any of their fields.

Using Default Values in the Blackboard

When you use a blackboard, you should set default values for each item in it so an application can assume the default values without having to set them each time it calls the trigger. Your default values should reflect what you want to happen when file modifications are performed by programs you didn't write. For example, what would you want a trigger to do when performing a CpyF (Copy File) command or a Data File Utility (DFU) procedure? For this blackboard example, I decided that the default action is to have the trigger perform the cross-reference file update.

Another reason to use default values is that, as a general rule, a trigger program should return without deactivating itself (i.e., without setting on LR in an RPG program) to avoid performance problems. This means a trigger could potentially remain activated after you're finished using it (especially in an interactive session). By using default values in the blackboard, you prevent some other application running later in the same interactive session from making erroneous assumptions about the initial values in the blackboard.

Figure C.4 shows excerpts from the trigger program that relate to default values in the blackboard.

FIGURE C.4

Implementing Default Values in the Sample Trigger Program

```
 .
 .
 .
D BlkBoard       DS                    Import              Ⓐ
D  ApplPgmName            10           Inz( 'NoPgm' )
D  UpdCustFlg              N           Inz( *On )
D  UpdItemFlg              N           Inz( *On )
D  OtherData             100           Inz( *ALL' ' )

D BoardInz       DS                    Import
D                         10           Inz( 'NoPgm' )
D                          N           Inz( *On )
D                          N           Inz( *On )
D                        100           Inz( *ALL' ' )
 .
 .
 .
```

```
 * Set the blackboard back to its initial value          Ⓑ
C                 Eval      BlkBoard = BoardInz

 * Terminate trigger - don't set on LR as this can cause
 * a performance penalty
C                 Return
 .
 .
 .
```

A /Copy directive causes the two data structures at **A** in Figure C.4 — the blackboard data structure (BlkBoard) and the initialization data structure (BoardInz) — to appear in the trigger program. Because BoardInz is used only to provide initial values, I don't bother giving names to its individual fields.

BoardInz contains the same number of fields as BlkBoard. Also, each field in BoardInz has the same type, length, and initial value as the corresponding field in BlkBoard. Just before the trigger program is terminated, it sets (via the Eval statement at **B**) the BlkBoard data structures back to their initial values. The two update flags (UpdCustFlg and UpdItemFlg) are always reset to *On. This means the default trigger action is to update the cross-reference files.

Conclusions

Blackboards aren't the only way to communicate additional information between an application and a trigger. For example, you might use a data area, a data queue, or even a normal database file. But these methods can't match the simplicity and elegance of a blackboard. Furthermore, these other techniques are slower because they require some type of system service to gain access.

For example, if you implement application/program communications with a data area, you must use the RPG In instruction. This approach requires RPG to retrieve the current value of the data area. (Using a data queue, user queue, or even a database file produces a similar situation.) But when you use a blackboard, the application and the trigger have access to the blackboard data at a speed similar to that with which they access their own local data.

So, if you ever need to pass more information between a trigger and an application than the trigger buffer provides, consider the blackboard technique.

Appendix D

ILE-Related Commands

Module Commands

ChgMod	Change Module
CrtCblMod	Create Cobol Module
CrtClMod	Create CL Module
CrtCMod	Create C Module
CrtRpgMod	Create RPG Module
DltMod	Delete Module
DspMod	Display Module
RtvBndSrc	Retrieve Binder Source
WrkMod	Work with Module

Program Commands

ChgPgm	Change Program
CrtBndC	Create Bound C Program
CrtBndCl	Create Bound CL Program
CrtBndRpg	Create Bound RPG Program
CrtPgm	Create Program
DltPgm	Delete Program
DspPgm	Display Program
DspPgmRef	Display Program References
UpdPgm	Update Program
WrkPgm	Work with Program

Service Program Commands

ChgSrvPgm	Change Service Program
CrtSrvPgm	Create Service Program
DltSrvPgm	Delete Service Program
DspSrvPgm	Display Service Program
UpdSrvPgm	Update Service Program
WrkSrvPgm	Work with Service Program

Binding Directory Commands

AddBndDirE	Add Binding Directory Entry
CrtBndDir	Create Binding Directory
DltBndDir	Delete Binding Directory
DspBndDir	Display Binding Directory
RmvBndDirE	Remove Binding Directory Entry
WrkBndDir	Work with Binding Directory
WrkBndDirE	Work with Binding Directory Entries

SQL-Related Commands

CrtSqlCI	Create SQL ILE C/400 Object
CrtSqlCbll	Create SQL ILE Cobol Object
CrtSqlRpgl	Create SQL ILE RPG Object

ILE Debugger Commands

DspModSrc	Display Module Source
EndDbg	End Debug Session
StrDbg	Start Debug Session

Binder Source Commands (Nonrunnable)

EndPgmExp	End Program Export
Export	Export
StrPgmExp	Start Program Export

Index

New Books in the 29th Street Press® and NEWS/400 Books™ Library

Creating CL Commands by Example

By Lynn Nelson

Learn from an expert how to create CL commands that have the same functionality and power as the IBM commands you use every day. You'll see how to create commands with all the function found in IBM's commands, including parameter editing, function keys, F4 prompt for values, expanding lists of values, and conditional prompting. Whether you're in operations or programming, *Creating CL Commands by Example* can help you tap the tremendous power and flexibility of CL commands to automate tasks and enhance applications. 134 pages.

DDS Keyword Reference

By James Coolbaugh

Reach for the *DDS Keyword Reference* when you need quick, at-your-fingertips information about DDS keywords for physical files, logical files, display files, printer files, and ICF files. In this no-nonsense volume, author Jim Coolbaugh gives you all the keywords you'll need, listed alphabetically in five sections. He explains each keyword, providing syntax rules and examples for coding the keyword. The *DDS Keyword Reference*, which is current to V4R3, is a friendly and manageable alternative to IBM's bulky DDS reference manual. 212 pages.

Domino R5 and the AS/400

By Justine Middleton, Wilfried Blankertz, Rosana Choruzy, Linda Defreyne, Dwight Egerton, Joanne Mindzora, Stephen Ryan, Juan van der Breggen, Felix Zalcmann, and Michelle Zolkos

Domino R5 and the AS/400 provides comprehensive installation and setup instructions for those installing Domino R5 "from scratch," upgrading from a previous version, or migrating from a platform other than the AS/400. In addition, you get detailed explanations of SMTP in Domino for AS/400, dial-up connectivity, directory synchronization, Advanced Services for Domino for AS/400, and Domino administration strategies, including backup strategies. 512 pages.

E-Business
Thriving in the Electronic Marketplace

By Nahid Jilovec

E-Business: Thriving in the Electronic Marketplace identifies key issues organizations face when they implement e-business projects and answers fundamental questions about entering and navigating the changing world of e-business. A concise guide to moving your business into the exciting world of collaborative e-business, the book introduces the four e-business models that drive today's economy and gives a clear summary of e-business technologies. It focuses on practical business-to-business applications. 172 pages.

Essentials of Subfile Programming
and Advanced Topics in RPG IV

By Phil Levinson

This textbook provides a solid background in AS/400 subfile programming in the newest version of the RPG language: RPG IV. Subfiles are the AS/400 tool that lets you display lists of data on the screen for user interaction. You learn to design and program subfiles, via step-by-step instructions and real-world programming exercises that build from chapter to chapter. A section on the Integrated Language Environment (ILE), introduced concurrently with RPG IV, presents tools and techniques that support effective modular programming. An instructor's kit is available. 293 pages.

Implementing Windows NT on the AS/400
Installing, Configuring, and Troubleshooting
By Nick Harris, Phil Ainsworth, Steve Fullerton, and Antoine Sammut

Implementing Windows NT on the AS/400: Installing, Configuring, and Troubleshooting provides everything you need to know about using NT on your AS/400, including how to install NT Server 4.0 on the Integrated Netfinity Server, synchronize user profiles and passwords between the AS/400 and NT, administer NT disk storage and service packs from the AS/400, back up NT data from the AS/400, manage NT servers on remote AS/400s, and run Windows-based personal productivity applications on the AS/400. 393 pages.

Introduction to AS/400 System Operations, Second Edition
By Heidi Rothenbuehler and Patrice Gapen

Here's the second edition of the textbook that covers what you need to know to become a successful AS/400 system operator or administrator. Updated through V4R3 of OS/400, *Introduction to AS/400 System Operations, Second Edition*, teaches you the basics of system operations so that you can manage printed reports, perform regularly scheduled procedures, and resolve end-user problems. New material covers the Integrated File System (IFS), AS/400 InfoSeeker, Operations Navigator, and much more. 182 pages.

Java and the AS/400
Practical Examples Using VisualAge for Java
By Daniel Darnell

This detailed guide takes you through everything you need to know about the AS/400's implementation of Java, including the QShell Interpreter and the Integrated File System (IFS), and development products such as VisualAge for Java (VAJ) and the AS/400 Toolbox for Java. The author provides several small application examples that demonstrate the advantages of Java programming for the AS/400. The companion CD contains all the sample code presented in the book and full-version copies of VAJ Professional Edition and the AS/400 Toolbox for Java. 300 pages.

Mastering the AS/400, Third Edition
A Practical, Hands-On Guide
By Jerry Fottral

This best-selling introduction to AS/400 concepts and facilities — fully updated for V4R3 of OS/400 — takes a utilitarian approach that stresses student participation. The book emphasizes mastery of system/user interface, member-object-library relationship, use of CL commands, basic database concepts, and program development utilities. The text prepares students to move directly into programming languages, database management, and system operations courses. Each lesson includes a lab that focuses on the essential topics presented in the lesson. 553 pages.

OPNQRYF by Example
By Mike Dawson and Mike Manto

The OPNQRYF (Open Query File) command is the single most dynamic and versatile command on the AS/400. Drawing from real-life, real-job experiences, the authors explain the basics and the intricacies of OPNQRYF with lots of examples to make you productive quickly. An appendix provides the UPDQRYF (Update Query File) command — a powerful addition to AS/400 and System/38 file update capabilities. 216 pages.

Programming in RPG IV, Second Edition
By Bryan Meyers and Judy Yaeger, Ph.D.

This textbook provides a strong foundation in the essentials of business programming, featuring the newest version of the RPG language: RPG IV. Focusing on real-world problems and down-to-earth solutions using the latest techniques and features of RPG, this book provides everything you need to know to write a well-designed RPG IV program. The second edition includes new chapters on defining data with D-specs and modular programming concepts, as well as an RPG IV summary appendix and an RPG IV style guide. An instructor's kit is available. 408 pages.

SQL/400 by Example

By James Coolbaugh

Designed to help you make the most of SQL/400, *SQL/400 by Example* includes everything from SQL syntax and rules to the specifics of embedding SQL within an RPG program. For novice SQL users, this book features plenty of introductory-level text and examples, including all the features and terminology of SQL/400. For experienced AS/400 programmers, *SQL/400 by Example* offers a number of specific examples that will help you increase your understanding of SQL concepts and improve your programming skills. 204 pages.

SQL/400 Developer's Guide

by Paul Conte and Mike Cravitz

SQL/400 Developer's Guide provides start-to-finish coverage of SQL/400, IBM's strategic language for the AS/400's integrated database. This textbook covers database and SQL fundamentals, SQL/400 Data Definition Language (DDL) and Data Manipulation Language (DML), and database modeling and design. Throughout the book, coding suggestions reinforce the topics covered and provide practical advice on how to produce robust, well-functioning code. Hands-on exercises reinforce comprehension of the concepts covered. 536 pages.

FOR A COMPLETE CATALOG OR TO PLACE AN ORDER, CONTACT

29th Street Press®
NEWS/400 Books™

Duke Communications International

221 E. 29th Street • Loveland, CO USA 80538-2727

(800) 650-1804 • (970) 663-4700 • Fax: (970) 663-4007

OR SHOP OUR WEB SITE: **www.as400networkstore.com**